MW01167097

Globalization Wisdom

The Seven Secrets of
Great Globalizers

Globalization Wisdom is a primer for the uninitiated and advanced outsourcing firm alike. Straightforward and forthright, it lays out the challenges to overcome not only to be effective at outsourcing, but also to leverage it to create truly strategic and differentiating capabilities.

Joshua Jewett, CIO, Family Dollar

This book is a must for any company or organization planning to launch or optimize their Globalization activities. Atul Vashistha continues to stand out as a globalization and outsourcing thought leader and expert. He points out the pitfalls, high lights best practices and provides advice which can help both beginners and veterans avoid costly mistakes and develop winning strategies.

Kenneth Hamel, SVP, SAP and Meeta Patel, VP, SAP

For well over a decade, the largest multinationals have turned to Atul Vashistha and his Neo Advisory team for guidance on globalization. When services globalization was questioned by politicians and the media, it was Atul who had the guts to take the questions and passionately defend the value of it. When multinationals looked to diversify their globalization risks, it was Atul who led the way in helping buyers and providers identify and establish service centers in developing countries around the globe. No surprise that Atul's book, Globalization Wisdom is the first hands-on guide for senior executives on what it takes to succeed in implementing a successful services globalization program. Leveraging seven secret tools for building shareholder value and competitive advantage, this book will be the defining source for services globalization for years to come.

Joseph Vales, Founder, Vales Consulting

As the globalization guru who went toe-to-toe with CNN's populist heavyweight Lou Dobbs and won, Atul Vashistha has extreme street cred in Flat World business circles. You'd be smart to read all seven of his lessons, take notes and quote him liberally in your slideware.

Jay Whitehead, Publisher, HRO Today, HRO Europe, FAO Today, CRO Magazines

Don't entertain globalization without it! And if you're en-route, read immediately!

Mike Faith, CEO, Headsets.com

This book delivers powerful strategic advice for the CEO and at the same time, delivers practical "how-to" tools for the teams that bring these strategies to life. Great take home value!

Bob Zollars, Chairman and CEO, Vocera Communications

Atul Vashistha is one of the most innovative and authoritative voices in the world of outsourcing. He brings clarity and focus to the most critical issues the industry faces. In Globalization Wisdom: The Seven Secrets of Great Globalizers, he offers the wisdom of the best in the business – most notably his own. This is 'must' reading for any executive currently outsourcing offshore or considering doing so in the future."

Catherine Allen, Chairman and CEO, The Santa Fe Group

Finally, one of globalization's true pioneers - Atul Vashistha - has distilled more than a decade of experience into a straight forward, invaluable guide to getting business right for the 21st century. A must read!"

Michael F. Corbett, Chairman and Founder, The International Association of Outsourcing Professionals (IAOP)

In Globalization Wisdom, Atul has done a great job sharing his unique insights on the secret ingredients companies need to win in today's globally competitive landscape.

Ed Mahoney, CIO, Micron

Atul is a pioneer in aiding buyers to make the most of their outsourcing relationships and has helped our organization implement sound governance principles. Globalization Wisdom brings this in depth experience and expertise to all of us.

Ed Kaywork, Director, Vendor Management, Humana

A critical "must read" handbook and resource for any CEO that is either engaged – or is preparing to expand globally.

Henry Dreifus, Founder & CEO, Dreifus Associates

Brilliant and immediately actionable! A must read for any executive who wants to improve their competitive position.

Mitch Lowe, Chairman & Founder, Jumpstart Automotive

I loved the Globalization Wisdom that Atul provides. Greatly needed! In an economy when companies struggle to lower costs and be innovative, many are leveraging globalization and sourcing to grow. This book provides keen insights from the well known global consultant and author and leaders in successful businesses on how to do so!

Alok Aggarwal, Founder & Chairman, Evalueserve

Globalization Wisdom gives the most comprehensive and holistic view yet on this important subject. I found in the book opportunities to explore, pitfalls to avoid and great examples to learn from.

Ashok Soota, Executive Chairman, MindTree

An extremely useful book from the foremost expert of globalization, Atul Vashistha, Globalization Wisdom, is a great read. The book shares years of experience of the author and leading companies on how to be great at leveraging globalization and outsourcing.

Ran J. Sharon, CEO Clariter Group BV

As a practitioner for over a decade, it was even more helpful to find these strategic and implementation ideas shared so well. Use Globalization Wisdom as your guide to managing and improving globalized operations.

Anu Gupta, Vice President, Profit and Process Improvement, Michaels Stores

Globalization is not just a concept; it is a reality. Sourcing globally is not just for a few savvy companies, it is a matter of fact. Atul has taken the concepts of globalization and has created a guide for thinkers as well as implementers. A guide for the next generation of business model.

Jagdish Dalal, President, JDalal Associates & Managing Director, Thought Leadership, IAOP

Vashistha's Globalization Wisdom illuminates a path to building sustainable competitive advantage both for your organization – and your career. Learning how to tap expertise worldwide is a business discipline worth learning even if it isn't yet taught in the leading business schools.

Rusty Weston, Founder of My Global Career and Third Set Media

I have been speaking, teaching and writing on services leadership for over three decades. As a new frontier, the globalization of services is an arena where innovation continues to blossom. Globalization Wisdom provides the formula for services innovation to business leaders crafted as a fun to read book with lively examples and dialogue.

Stephen Brown, Edward M. Carson Chair, Professor of Marketing and Executive Director, Center for Services Leadership, W.P. Carey School of Business, Arizona State University

A must read for organizations and leaders to succeed in today's challenging global economy. Atul's passion, commitment and vast experiences, along with many stories/case studies, make this book realistic and insightful. A great tool and road map to help you sustain competitive advantage!

Julia Santos, Director, Head of Worldwide Strategic Outsourcing, Johnson & Johnson Group of Consumer Companies.

Atul was a great resource for our company. His knowledge of why to outsource, where to outsource, how to go about outsourcing, and how to continue managing an outsourced operation were paramount in our decision making process. Within the first few interactions, it was evident that Atul knew what he was taking about and was more than willing to share his thoughts. Globalization Wisdom brings this to all in an easy to digest book.

John G. Allen, G&A Partners

Globalization Wisdom and Atul Vashistha have truly captured the 'Good to Great' for Globalization and Outsourcing. The skills and tools that can be applied from this will become increasingly more important in enabling businesses to compete and prosper in a global economy."

Steve Church, Senior Vice President, Chief Operational Excellence Officer, Avnet

Atul Vashistha is a recognized guru in globalizing services for over a decade. He and his teams have advised numerous Global 2000 firms in their globalization effort. Now, his second book, Globalization Wisdom, helps us all by providing a practical guide to globalization success, a must-read for companies thinking or going global. Walter Fang, President of Neusoft America

On the leading edge. Again. Atul's keen insights into Globalization will push your thinking well beyond traditional Outsourcing and Offshoring. It's an easy read, filled with new ideas and great tips on how to leverage the very best from around the world.

Linda Tuck Chapman, President, ONTALA Performance Solutions

There is a Chinese "red Thread" woven through Atul's advice on Globalization. People must be equipped with the core competencies to do their jobs seamlessly across 'cultures.' Culture can be defined in many ways – corporate, nation-state, function, gender, etc. – but in the end, the people we select to work on these global initiatives must be, to quote Atul, "agile, understand change and are globally savvy." In my work enabling the human factor of global execution for client companies, 'globally savvy' can also be expressed as 'Globally Fluent.' In other words, one's ability to read their cultural counterpart, to understand the 'why' behind their behavior, and get back to work. Atul's 7 secrets speak well to the critical importance of enabling the human interaction across cultures en route to successfully achieving the global workstreams that drive globalization excellence.

Dave Eaton, Co-Founder & Former President, Aperian Global

Fantastic guide for next generation business leaders on how to navigate in a Global economy. Must read for leaders trying to improve Global leadership skills.

Steve Bandrowczak, Former CIO, Lenovo

In Globalization Wisdom, Atul shares his knowledge in a structured and easy-to-follow approach. This 'how-to' book is a thorough education for anyone new to outsourcing as well as a very helpful reminder and reference tool for experts.

Christopher A Long, EVP and General Manager, LifeMasters

Globalization Wisdom

The Seven Secrets of Great Globalizers

ATUL VASHISTHA

Global Business Press

San Francisco, USA

Bangalore, India

Dedications

I am delighted to dedicate Globalization Wisdom: The 7 Secrets of Great Globalizers, my second book to my clients and business leaders who made me dig deeper, probe further and thus finally develop better answers. I would like to especially thank

- Ron Kifer
- Wim Elfrink
- Rob Carter
- Steve Bandrowzcak
- Ken Kennappan
- Mitch Klaif
- Michael Corbett
- Eugene Kublanov
- John Hartmann
- Mike Zeigler
- Tom Waller
- Gary Schneider
- Roshan Nambiyattil
- Joe Vales

- Ross Docksey
- Lou Dobbs
- Michael Bayer
- Mark Rosman
- Stephen Brown
- Robert Manschot
- Avinash Vashistha
- Tito Yuchengo
- Kathy White
- Meeta Patel
- Henry Dreifus
- YPOers
- Sandeep Karoor
- Jay Kerley

- Jorge Muxica
- Craig Ostrander
- Josh Day
- Madhu Akkaraju
- Shom Biswas
- Gaurav Garg
- Will Whitehorn
- Michael Corbett
- Mike Faith
- Shalabh Garg,
- Govind Maheshwari,
- Keerthi Kumar

You make globalization work!

Many others helped inspire this book and I thank you.

I especially want to dedicate this book to my wife, Jodie and daughter, Tia who inspire me to "make a difference".

Atul Vashistha

.

Contents

Introduction:
The Multiple Rewards of Successful Globalization

Continual technological, social and economic advancements propel us further into a global business world in which business executives in Boise, Idaho can teleconference with business executives in Beijing, China as if they were sitting across the table from each other. Entire departments now work remotely from home offices and other locations as the rule rather than the exception. And with the cropping up of freelance online employment markets such as Elance, Live Work and ODesk that serve as intermediaries between businesses and services workers, the ability to globalize is more accessible to businesses and individuals of all sizes.

The initial wave of globalization in the late 1990s and early 2000s was about taking advantage of lower labor costs in offshore destinations. With the rapid, inexpensive transmission of data available, businesses can leverage the time zone difference with locations like India, China and Malaysia to achieve 24-hour workdays. But these opportunities are only the beginning of what services globalization offers. Today's successful globalizers understand that there are a number of additional advantages to services globalization and embrace them whereas other not so successful leaders do not. Furthermore, they understand that they can't afford *not* to.

Successfully implemented, globalization can be a means for shoring up competitive advantage as organizations take advantage not only of lower labor costs but also diverse intellectual capabilities, growth and quality enhancement opportunities, as well as the ability to get products to market more quickly. Successful globalizers that embrace a global and flexible mentality are constantly looking for opportunities to improve—whether those opportunities present themselves in Michigan, Mexico, Malaysia, or anywhere in between. Much more than bottom-line labor costs and longer workdays, successful globalization means a more successful business, period.

Some organizations and leaders have leveraged those opportunities successfully. Most have not. Successful globalizers realize—while many not so successful organizations and leaders do not—that services globalization is not a one-shot deal. It is still a relatively new way of doing business; a new part of the business lifecycle that requires not only diligent planning, but also ongoing management. And it requires strong commitment from the organization's leadership.

Not surprisingly, the companies and leaders that are successful globalizers engage in similar practices—key practices that other companies regardless of size can emulate. In my two decades of consulting to major corporations on global sourcing I've seen similar trends and patterns among firms that have succeeded in services globalization and have come to recognize that there are seven best practices in successful services globalization. This book is about sharing those practices, these seven secrets.

The seven chapters that follow expound the key attitudes and behaviors that successful globalizers share—and offer concrete guides for replicating their success within your own organization. I've paired what I know from my work with Neo Advisory (Formerly neoIT), as an advisor to firms looking to globalize their services, with sage advice and stories from executives at organizations that are successful globalizers, many of whom were among the first to globalize services, including Applied Materials, Lenovo, Virgin, Cisco, FedEx and Plantronics. The end result is a book designed specifically for C-level executives and practitioners at organizations positioned at all stages of global maturity.

What or Who is a Successful Globalizer?

Being a successful globalizer is not a black-and-white distinction, but when referring to successful globalizers, they tend to be companies and leaders that rank highly on a number of factors, including:

- Variety of services globalized

- Number of suppliers leveraged

- Scale of global operations

- Geographical distribution of global operations

- Variety of client-supplier relationship models leveraged

- Number of years of global sourcing experience

- Growth in global sourcing activities

- Innovation in global sourcing models

In 2006, Neo Advisory (Formerly neoIT) conducted a research study to determine just how many of *Fortune* magazine's 500 largest companies are highly active in services globalization. Based on the factors listed above, we found that 27 (5%) of the *Fortune* 500 companies have high levels of global maturity. Of those 27 firms, 18 were among the 100 largest companies. Table 1 offers more detail about how the *Fortune* 500 companies fare in terms of global maturity.

Table 1: Global Maturity by Company Size

Fortune 500 ranking	Global maturity level			
	Very low/ none	Low	Medium	High
1–100	5	20	57	18
101–200	15	22	60	3
201–300	16	45	38	1
301–400	21	46	31	2
401–500	31	37	29	3
Total	88 (18%)	170 (34%)	215 (43%)	27 (5%)

Source: Neo Advisory (Formerly neoIT)

In this case, Neo Advisory's analysis focused on large firms—those on *Fortune*'s list of the 500 largest companies. But successful globalizers are by no means relegated to the ranks of the largest firms. And by walking in the footsteps of these successful large firms, services globalization can benefit smaller firms as well.

Why Globalize?

Neo Advisory's 2006 research into the global activity of *Fortune* magazine's 500 largest companies found that the most financially successful companies are engaged in higher levels of services globalization than less successful companies. Specifically:

A majority of Fortune 500 companies engage in services globalization.

Of the *Fortune* 500 companies, more than 80% have engaged services globalization to some degree; that group is led by the technology and banking, financial services and insurance (BFSI) industries, in which more than 90% of companies have engaged in services globalization. Companies in the infrastructure industry (including the transportation and logistics, energy and utilities, and real estate sectors) have the lowest levels of globalization engagement overall, with only 74% of companies engaging in services globalization.

Companies that globalize services create more value for shareholders.

Companies highly engaged in services globalization increased shareholder value three times more than companies in the market overall. Among companies in the Neo Advisory (Formerly neoIT) Services Globalization Index, shareholder value increased 41.3% between January, 2004 and January, 2006. Among companies in the S&P 500, shareholder value increased 13.1% in the same period. Figure 1 demonstrates that quite remarkable difference in shareholder values.

Figure 1: Growth in Shareholder Value, 2004-2006

Source: Neo Advisory (Formerly neoIT)

Figure 1 also reveals that the gap in shareholder value growth between the Neo Advisory Services Globalization Index and the S&P 500 has grown over time. Why? As companies' services globalization initiatives continue to develop, the impact of those initiatives on shareholder value multiplies.

Companies that globalize services are more profitable.

In 2005, profitability at companies that were highly engaged in services globalization was 15%. At companies that were not engaged, or engaged at a very low level, profitability was 6.5%—8.5% lower than at highly globalized companies. Especially in industries where profit margins are razor-thin, an 8.5% profitability difference can put a company above the competitive edge or far below it in today's economy.

Mapping *Fortune* 500 companies according to their levels of global maturity and profitability, it's clear that the most successful globalizers—those companies with high levels of global maturity—have the highest levels of profitability as well. Companies with medium levels of global maturity have medium levels of profitability and companies with low levels of global maturity have low levels of profitability.

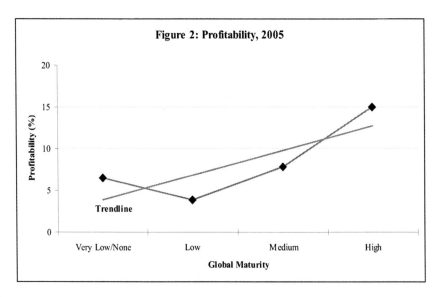

Figure 2: Profitability, 2005

Source: Neo Advisory (Formerly neoIT)

Contrary to expectations, however, those companies with very low or no global maturity did not have the lowest levels of profitability. Instead, it was the companies in the low global maturity category that had the lowest overall levels of profitability.

There are a number of plausible explanations for that unexpected result: The companies with very low or no global maturity have higher levels of profitability than their global maturity would suggest because of superior products, market monopolies or position in a sunrise industry, or perhaps their high relative profitability led them toward complacency with regard to services globalization.

One factor which may result in lower-than-expected levels of profitability among companies with low levels of global maturity is the fact that many companies that see globalization as a cost-cutting opportunity and nothing more are only driven to globalize because of burgeoning costs—costs which, in the initial stages of the companies' globalization initiative could still be driving down profitability. Nevertheless, there is a very clear trend overall of increasing profitability as global maturity increases.

BFSI companies that globalize see higher revenue growth.

Among all Fortune 500 BFSI companies, revenue growth between 2004 and 2005 was, on average, 16.1%. Highly globalized BFSI companies saw revenue growth of 23.8%—7.7% higher than the average and 14.3% higher than BFSI companies with very low or no global maturity.

In the banking, financial services, and insurance industry, revenue growth generally increases as global maturity increases. Yet across all other industries, revenue growth numbers do not follow that expected pattern.

It makes sense that a positive correlation between globalization and revenue growth would be the last to appear among the three performance metrics we've analyzed. That's because it's more difficult for companies to achieve higher levels of revenue growth than to achieve increased shareholder value and increased profitability.

It also makes sense that companies in the BFSI industry would be the first to realize that positive correlation between globalization and revenue growth—because many of the early adopters of services globalization fall into that industry group. Yet the fact that the BFSI industry has been the first to see increased revenue growth alongside successful globalization doesn't preclude other industries from following.

Table 2: Revenue Growth, 2005

	Global maturity level				
	Very low/ none	Low	Medium	High	All levels
Infrastructure	26.4	19.5	19.9	N/A	21.5
BFSI	9.5	16.0	16.0	23.8	16.1
Manufacturing	25.6	14.0	9.3	5.0	13.5
Technology	14.2	5.2	15.2	14.5	12.6
Healthcare and life sciences	13.7	15.2	4.7	7.2	9.3
Others	13.4	2.9	8.7	3.1	8.9
Retail	8.8	9.5	6.8	N/A	8.0
All industries	**18.9**	**13.5**	**12.1**	**12.1**	**13.7**

Source: Neo Advisory

While the evidence linking outstanding financial performance with high levels of global maturity doesn't prove that engaging services globalization causes a company's performance to improve, it does offer a very clear statement about the benefits that successful globalizers are enjoying—including dramatically faster growth in shareholder value, higher levels of profitability, and for the BFSI industry, revenue growth.

That doesn't mean it's time to put down this book and jump on the globalization bandwagon. The companies enjoying the rewards of globalization are *successful* globalizers—those that have done the hard work required to create successful global sourcing engagements, not those that blindly source IT or business processes domestically or to Canada, India, Mexico, China, Brazil, South Africa or Hungary.

It does mean that there's a very real benefit to reading this book and learning how to help your organization become one of those successful globalizers.

Road Map

Perhaps one of the most fundamental secrets of successful globalizers is that services globalization, like most business initiatives, is a lot about planning, trying, learning and retrying. By understanding the paths that other organizations have taken to become successful globalizers, the learning curve on your own path will hopefully be shorter.

In the course of this book, we'll share the following seven secrets to successful globalizers:

Secret #1: Embrace Globalization

Secret #2: Welcome Globalization as a Transformation Lever

Secret #3: Adopt a Lifecycle Approach

Secret #4: Align Business and Globalization Objectives

Secret #5: Assign the Best People

Secret #6: Implement a Strong Governance Model

Secret #7: Embrace a Continuous Improvement Mindset

Secret #1:

Embrace Globalization

Secret #1: Embrace Globalization

Successful globalizers understand that there may be other advantages besides cost savings in sourcing to other countries, including improved quality, growth opportunities, faster time to market and the ability to focus on core functions. They consider every corner of the world as a potential sourcing destination, thinking about the unique advantages and disadvantages that each location offers.

Fifteen or twenty years ago services globalization wasn't really a concept that most had thought of yet. The first globalizers sourced processes to developing nations largely to take advantage of lower wage rates in countries like India and called it offshore outsourcing.

But that, of course, is yesterday's news, as Ron Kifer, Group Vice President and Chief Information Officer (CIO) of Applied Materials puts it. In the fifteen or twenty years since the first globalizers ventured across the sea with their information technology (IT) and business processes, the concept has evolved. Today's successful globalizers have learned that there are other advantages besides cost savings involved in sourcing to other countries. And as offshore destinations like India and the Philippines have evolved their Information Technology Outsourcing (ITO) and Business Process Outsourcing (BPO) industries, companies have realized that there are also quality advantages in sourcing to those and other destinations.

One underlying fact successful globalizers understand is that services globalization has come a long way from offshore outsourcing and continues to evolve every day. As services globalization evolves, new opportunities arise. The reality, as Kifer sees it, is that a company can embrace, leverage and be a part of that globalization or it can become its victim.

"It's greatly important that global organizations understand that we're moving to a globalized economy and understand that they have to have the flexibility to be able to do the work wherever the work is more cost-effectively done and wherever the work is high-touch to the customer. That's why we're pushing globalization as a key strategic initiative in our organization because we want to be on the leading edge of that," Kifer explains.

That concept of flexibility—of being open to new opportunities—leads into the first secret of successful globalizers: Embrace globalization. Successful globalizers welcome services globalization into their organizations with open arms; they allow themselves to be constantly learning, constantly open to the new opportunities—and challenges—that the evolution of services globalization presents. Embracing globalization means looking at the big picture; considering every corner of the world as a potential sourcing destination and thinking about the unique advantages and opportunities that each location offers.

Embracing globalization is also an important stepping-stone in the development of a services globalization strategy. Whatever may come, organizations must be always mindful that they are embracing globalization for all that it may offer.

Model for Embracing Globalization

The basic model for embracing globalization has four components:

1) Embrace globalization across the business.

2) Ask whether your processes should be performed better elsewhere.

3) Mandate the globalization of processes that can be performed better elsewhere.

4) Keep an eye on the future.

Component #1: Embrace Globalization Across the Business

When the offshore outsourcing trend first caught hold of U.S. businesses, most firms saw it as an opportunity to reduce costs through labor arbitrage. But as the movement has evolved—as offshore outsourcing has become services globalization—companies have looked past cost considerations.

In fact, flexibility is even more important than cost in services globalization. "If cost was your primary consideration, I think that you're going to fall short of meeting the real objectives," Kifer says.

"The real objective of a sound globalization strategy is to have a flexible workforce and global model and to realize that the markets, customers and competitive environment is going to change, which will require a company to maintain competitiveness to be able to do work in a different model in a different place over time," he adds. And *that's* why successful globalizers embrace it across the business.

Component #2: Ask Why It Cannot be Done Elsewhere

Bill Gates, Co-Founder of Microsoft, once said that, "If we are not realistic about what we're good at, then there is a chance of going backwards in the face of further competition." In asking why each process cannot be done elsewhere, an organization must be realistic about which processes are a) core competencies and b) performed most efficiently in-house.

There's no room for egoism in this process: to survive, a business must be willing to strip itself bare, down to only those processes that are true core competencies. Every business function should be on the table for globalization until it's taken off, and only because it can be performed most efficiently in-house domestically.

Steve Bandrowczak, former Lenovo and Nortel CIO, has extensive globalization experience both currently and with his past work with Avnet and DHL. "At all those companies," he told me, "moving any process that was non-customer-facing to a low-cost, highly efficient part of the world was imperative."

For successful globalizers, it's not only the full range of processes that can be globalized, but also the locations that are up for consideration. Bandrowczak says that U.S. firms are often wary of developing countries. "They say, 'I'd like to go to China, but there are aspects of doing business there that make me nervous.'" Bandrowczak eschews that kind of risk aversion. "You're not really a global company unless you're playing in one of the largest, fastest growing economies in the world."

Component #3: Mandate It

Mandating the globalization of processes that cannot be done elsewhere is an important part of stripping an organization bare. Within a company, some people will resist globalization. Successful globalizers neither back down from that resistance nor tolerate it. Effective change management that secures top-level commitment and buy-in and addresses points of resistance is a critical part of a successful globalization initiative.

Executives at Virgin have not only mandated globalization, but they have built it in to the fabric of their enterprise. Will Whitehorn, President of Virgin Galactic, says that one of the secrets of Virgin's success is that it's organized like a branded private equity venture capital firm. "We don't really run companies," he explains. "We take stake in companies and then we let them leverage the Virgin brand."

In that way, Virgin is simultaneously global and incredibly local. At the brand level, they have fully embraced globalization. At the decision-making level, their actions are very local. They're a global brand that leverages local opportunities, opportunities that are close to the customer.

Component #4: Keep an Eye on the Future

Companies must be constantly vigilant and always prepared to scrap the old way of doing business to take advantage of new opportunities. It used to be that to engage in this sort of flexibility made companies leaders. Today it is a business imperative. As Thomas Friedman wrote in *The World is Flat*, "If you want to grow and flourish in a flat world, you better learn how to change and align yourself with it."

Bandrowczak says that having a vision for the end-state of any globalization initiative is critical, and it "has to be better than the pain you go through to get there." "In other words," he explains, "if you set a vision saying this is where we need to be, this is why we need to be there, and this is why it's going to be better than the state we're in today, then people have a better understanding and are less resistant to that change."

How Others Have Embraced Globalization

Companies that have embraced globalization, including leading companies such as GE, Aviva, Texas Instruments, Google and Proctor & Gamble, have found large pools of productive labor in offshore destinations. But they have found something more in offshore employees as well: top engineering talent, attention to detail and quality, sophisticated mid-level and senior-level management, and even a level of brand identity and loyalty that rivals that of their domestic employees.

A leading Fortune 500 bank offers a good example of a successful globalizer and early first-mover. The company's business objectives include business operations in many geographies with a variety of business functions in its portfolio, including leading technology adoption and pioneering banking standards; rapidly expanding business in terms of customer base and business transactions; continuously innovating processes; and living up to customer service expectations.

The company was one of the earliest pioneers to adopt services globalization. Its strategy evolved from sourcing for lower costs to sourcing for higher quality. Through its evolution, the company has adopted a variety of global business models—including joint venture, captive center, and third party—to expand its services globalization footprint. This bank has been a success story in this tough economy.

In addition to the variety of business models the company has adopted, it has also created sourcing relationships in a number of different global destinations, testament to the company's portfolio approach to services globalization. The basic principle behind a portfolio approach is that each destination has a number of particular competencies, as well as a number of particular risks. By sourcing to a variety of countries, each with a different set of competencies and risks, the company can maximize the benefits of its total sourcing strategy and minimize its risks.

This Fortune 500 firm has embraced globalization not only by adopting the portfolio approach to globalization, but also by considering every process that could be done more efficiently, for less money and at a higher level of quality, and in a different destination. Indeed, the firm has globalized a number of functions across its business, including front-, middle-, and back-office operations.

The Importance of Visionary Leaders Who Embrace Globalization

The most successful globalizers are companies who have visionary leaders at their helms. Steve Bandrowczak says that trying to succeed in globalization without visionary leaders is like trying to bake a delicious cake with stale ingredients. "I don't care how you mix it," he explains, "you're going to come out with a bad cake."

Instead, he urges that "Good companies—high-velocity, high-change companies— either have good change leaders or have to go out and get them and put them in the right positions. You've got to be able to get the right management, get the right change leaders and change agents in place. And many companies don't do that.

They try to put these programs in place using the legacy management team, and they come up with the same stale results."

Visionary leaders—the ones at the helm of globalization since the beginning of globalization—saw the big picture as it emerged: how the playing field expanded from the U.S. and Western Europe to encompass India, the Philippines, China, Ireland, Poland, Chile, Brazil, Russia, South Africa, and more. These visionary leaders understood, even in the early days of globalization, that global sourcing would become a key competitive advantage. They saw that global sourcing could not only allow them to reduce their costs, but it could also allow them to grow more quickly, to cut time to market, and even to improve efficiency and raise quality levels.

Jack Welch, GE's former chief executive, was certainly one of those visionary leaders. You'll notice more than a few references to him throughout this book. That's because GE has been one of the most successful globalizers and was one of the principal early-movers in services globalization. Jack Welch himself has been a leader in the evolution of services globalization.

Welch summarized how he saw globalization during his period of leadership at GE: "Globalization has changed us [GE] into a company that searches the world, not just to sell or to source, but to find intellectual capital—the world's best talent and greatest ideas." Welch clearly embraces services globalization as a means of labor arbitrage as well as a way to take advantage of new pools of intellectual capital and talent. Welch made the world his playground, so to speak, by completely opening the company to search every corner of the world for new and better opportunities.

Indeed, GE is a good example of a company that has successfully embraced globalization. Responding in part to potential clients that had expressed interest in partnering with Gecis (GE Capital International Services) to streamline their global operations, GE commercialized Gecis in late 2004. Gecis is now Genpact, a leading third-party supplier of technology-enabled business processes with operations centers in over ten countries including United States, Mexico, Hungary, Romania, Chile, China and India.

When GE saw an opportunity to expand its global services operations, it took it— even though that meant divesting a majority stake in Gecis (GE retained a 40% stake in the company). It's that type of enduring flexibility and ability to forget all of yesterday's rules to take advantage of today's opportunities that continues to mark GE as a leading embracer of globalization.

Embracing globalization is the first secret of successful globalizers not because it is necessarily the most important, but because it lays the foundation for the six secrets that follow. Indeed, we'll see the principles that underlie this first secret pop up throughout the next chapters.

Embracing globalization is about seeing the big picture. It's about looking beyond a single destination or a particular set of processes. It's about an attitude change;

about bringing the principles of services globalization into the business and embracing them in every decision that's made.

That attitude change was once the key to competitive advantage—for early first-movers like GE, Lenovo, Applied Materials, Virgin, and the Fortune 500 bank. But as services globalization continues to evolve and as more businesses begin to adopt services globalization than ever before, globalization becomes less and less a competitive advantage and more and more a business necessity.

Secret #1: Embrace Globalization: Key Points

- Successful globalizers understand that there are other advantages besides cost savings in sourcing to other countries, including improved quality, better time to market, growth opportunities, and the ability to focus on core functions.

- Embracing globalization means looking at the big picture—considering every corner of the world as a potential sourcing destination and understanding the unique advantages and opportunities that each location offers.

- The basic model for embracing globalization has four components:

    - **Embracing globalization across the business.** The globalization of services should not necessarily be relegated to back-office processes or IT. Every business function should be on the table for globalization until it's taken off because it can be performed most efficiently in-house.

    - **Asking why your processes can or cannot be performed elsewhere.** To survive, a business must be willing to strip itself bare, down to only those processes that are truly core competencies.

    - **Mandating the globalization of processes that can be performed elsewhere.** Within a company, some people will resist globalization. Successful globalizers neither back down from that resistance nor tolerate it.

    - **Keeping an eye on the future.** Companies must be constantly vigilant and always prepared to scrap the old way of doing business to take advantage of new opportunities.

Secret #2:

Welcome Globalization As a Transformation Lever

Secret #2: Welcome Globalization as a Transformation Lever

Enabling business transformation through globalization is one way that successful globalizers leverage services globalization to create competitive advantage. They:

1) Generate solid leadership commitment

2) Develop new organizational designs and structures

3) Collaboratively map out and execute change management

4) Communicate effectively

5) Educate and develop new competencies

6) Redesign existing business processes

Services globalization should now constitute an important part of the strategic plan of any firm. As I have said before, if your three-year or even one-year business plan doesn't include the globalization of services, throw it out and rewrite it or you'll be written off. That may sound harsh, but in today's competitive business world services globalization is no longer an option that a few elite companies take; it is a business imperative for any company that wishes to survive and flourish, especially in this economy.

As discussed in Chapter 1, services globalization is much more than offshore outsourcing. It is the complete embracing of cross-border operations as a means to reduce costs, improve quality, and enable business growth. It is also a means for business transformation.

And that's the second secret of successful globalizers: Welcome globalization as a transformation lever. Companies that have really embraced the idea of globalization as a transformation lever see it as a way to do business differently. They use it as a lever to, for example, change the way they keep in touch with their customers, launch new products, and even treat their employees.

Successful globalizers see that globalization is about more than cost savings and they ask themselves: What can globalization do for my business in addition to reducing costs? How can I leverage it to build competitive advantage? Once they figure out the answer, they act quickly to realize it.

A few years ago, Electronic Arts (EA) began to realize that they needed innovation from outside the U.S. to address increasingly large client bases in Asian and European markets. They asked: How do I grow my business in Asia where the typical U.S.-type PC console mode doesn't work? Globalization, for them, was about addressing the market in a whole different way. Now, they have facilities in China and India and leverage partners in Ukraine, Vietnam, China, India, Russia and other such locations.

Plantronics CEO Ken Kannappan told me how he looks for the unique advantages that each potential location will offer. "Europe, for example, is at the forefront of Bluetooth® technology, so that's where we develop those products. China is a far more cost-effective location for some processes, compared to California, so we have functions done there, too. It's natural to get those competency centers where you can get a rich trove of talent of the most cost-effective process." I heard similar stories from Yahoo, Oracle and Google engineering executives.

In taking the following six critical steps, successful globalizers like Plantronics and EA allow for the full realization of globalization as a transformation lever. They:

1) Generate solid leadership commitment

2) Develop a new organizational design and structure

3) Collaboratively map out and execute change management

4) Communicate effectively

5) Educate and develop new competencies

6) Redesign business processes.

Critical Step #1: Generate Solid Leadership Commitment

Generating solid leadership commitment is the first critical step in realizing the transformative aspect of globalization. A successful business transformation—especially one as highly visible and potentially disruptive as globalization—requires the cooperation, buy-in, and commitment of an organization's employees, from the top to the bottom.

If the organization's own leaders do not buy in to the change, lower-level employees likely won't either. A committed transformation leader will provide strategic direction and set executive expectations; identify and assign owners to the respective transformation areas; act as a conduit in championing the initiative to other functional areas; and keep the transformation on the executive agenda.

One of the important functions of leadership commitment is to provide an example for lower-level employees of the cooperative, encouraging attitudes that the organization requires. Another important function of leadership commitment is the facilitation of process approvals. Because the globalization of services is often a large undertaking, the elimination of bureaucracy within the process is important.

Clearly defined leadership expectations and authority help to cut through that bureaucracy.

Genpact, formerly Gecis, succeeded in its global business transformation initiatives in part because of the solid leadership commitment and buy-in that started at the top with CEO Jack Welch. Gecis began in India as a small operation and became one of the largest offshore operations in the world. Early on, top-level managers created a governance team with clearly defined strategic and tactical objectives to guide Gecis in its transformation process. Eventually the governance team, still fully supported by top-level management, expanded its focus to include increasing the company's operational complexity. It was that type of enduring commitment, combined with the leadership mandate handed down from the top that allowed Gecis to leverage services globalization as a business transformation agent and be the successful global services firm, Genpact, today.

Critical Step #2: Develop a New Organizational Design and Structure

The second critical step in leveraging globalization as a business transformation agent is to develop a new organizational design and structure, considering what the organization's new operating structure will look like as it develops globally. Specifically, the organization must define the new roles for the global delivery centers and redefine the roles for existing centers—developing new operating models that account for new jobs and work structures, performance management systems and governance teams.

The four key steps to develop a new organizational design and structure are:

1) Develop an operating model in line with the organization's future direction.

2) Define roles and responsibilities within the new structure.

3) Develop delivery models that leverage new offshore operations to improve the organization's value proposition.

4) Identify the necessary governance organization and develop clear responsibilities.

HSBC Holdings plc (HSBC) is a good example of an organization that developed a new organizational design and structure in order to facilitate its global business transformation. Six years after opening its first offshore operating centers in China, HSBC had established offshore operations in ten Asian countries. That globalization was coordinated by a group called the Global Processing Team, which evolved from a small team reporting to the company's UK Senior Manager for Personal Financial Services to a strategic division of its own that reports directly to the Group CEO.

The emergence of an overarching governance group to guide HSBC in its newly expanded global endeavors—and the flexible expansion of the group itself—

allowed HSBC to take full advantage of the business transformation opportunities presented by the company's globalization.

Critical Step #3: Collaboratively Map Out and Execute Change Management

Sometimes called "transition planning" or more recently "change coping," change management is the third critical step to successful business transformation. Here, change management involves helping existing team members to become resilient, enable knowledge transfer, engage resource planning and communicate.

One important function of the change management team is to ensure that the transformation is mapped out and executed collaboratively—with all stakeholders actively involved in the process. In addition, a successful change management process will identify sponsors, change architects and stakeholders and ensure that all are prepared for the change and have effective roles. A critical part of this change is to help the stakeholders be positive, focused, flexible, organized and proactive.

As they undertook global sourcing and transformation, leaders like P&G not only focused on effective knowledge transfer but also worked to ensure that 99.5% of their affected staff was placed with the outsourcers or alternate employers. Other firms such as Schneider Electric made sure that cultural training was done at both ends to enhance mutual understanding and collaboration.

Mitch Klaif, CIO, Time Inc., likens change management and adoption to quicksand. As he address any new change, he always likes to think whether this change is like quicksand, i.e., if you go slow, you'll get past it but if you move fast, you could sink.

Critical Step #4: Communicate Effectively

Effective communication is the fourth critical step to successful business transformation. It involves planning for the human impact of the change and identifying potential points of resistance as well as developing a plan to accommodate that impact and deal with that resistance. Effective communication will focus on an organization's internal stakeholders, though external communications may be important as well—especially when the business change involves a highly visible, socially divisive topic like globalization.

Targeted communication with various stakeholder groups and communicating through the most appropriate channels is important. In most cases, highly personal communication (such as small-group meetings) is preferable. Developing key messaging is also important; employees, for example, will want to hear about how the transformation will affect the company as a whole as well as how it will affect them individually.

Some companies have also found it beneficial to communicate transformation plans with their external customers. For example, E-Loan, an online lender, discloses the details of its offshore processing program—as well as its benefits, including faster processing time—to potential customers, who can then choose to have their application processed offshore or domestically. In late 2004, E-Loan said that 87% of its customers selected the offshore option.

E-Loan found that by communicating effectively, openly and honestly that it built trust relationships with its clients and it educated them on the benefits of services globalization, in turn allowing the company to reap the cost savings and other benefits it had envisioned for its global business transformation.

Critical Step #5: Educate and Develop New Competencies

Services globalization opens up a lot of new economic, legal, political and cultural frontiers, especially for the organization that has not globalized its services before. To effectively navigate those frontiers, an organization must take the fifth critical step in leveraging globalization as a transformation agent: educate its onshore employees as well as its new global partners. An organization should begin that education process by identifying the training needs and developing a training curriculum for both the existing onshore and the new global organizations.

One of the important benefits of services globalization—and one of the aspects that can enable globalization as a transformation lever—is the ability for employees at onsite locations to develop new competencies and move to higher value-added positions. But often those employees need additional training to assume those new responsibilities.

A successful globalizing organization will define a training approach and align it with a career development plan for employees that will be retrained in new competencies. Leading firms such as American Express ensure that the new relationship manager roles are grown from within through training and on-the-job training.

Many times, an organization will find that it must also provide training for its new global partners. Exult (now merged with Hewitt) is a good example of an organization that has successfully trained new global partners within a global business transformation process. In 2002, Exult, which had already been outsourcing some of its IT requirements, decided to globalize its business processes as well.

The company found that it could not only achieve cost savings through global business process delivery, but that it could also tap into new sources of skill while maintaining the high level of quality and skill that the company's customers had come to expect. It also found another benefit: that by being close to large pools of lower-cost talent, it could more easily accommodate its global growth. To enable the realization of those benefits, Exult set up training programs for its new offshore hires and implemented a westernization, voice-coaching, and accent-coaching program.

In many cases, the transformative opportunity in globalization is the ability to focus on core competencies. Group VP and CIO Ron Kifer explains that globalization allowed Applied Materials to transform his organization, by becoming focused on those core competencies that added competitive value.

"Services globalization provides us with the opportunity to take all those me-too capabilities that don't add any value to the business and move them to where they can be most effectively supplied, where we can take advantage of the more mature processes, metrics and capabilities of our strategic partners and refocus our entire internal team on real value-added core competencies," he says.

Lenovo does the same. Former CIO Steve Bandrowczak adds, "As we looked at moving our infrastructure and moving our functions, we also looked at the ways our functions worked, making sure that they were adding value and that we were not doing things that were redundant or non-value-adding simply because we had been doing them that way for twenty years."

Critical Step #6: Redesign Processes

The final critical step that successful globalizers take to realize the transformative potential of services globalization is process redesign. In a successful business transformation, processes are redesigned to include automation, new onshore/offshore interactions, knowledge management and other support systems.

Because globalization increases the complexity of an organization's business networks it is vital that those networks be optimally managed to ensure the highest level of efficiency in the delivery cycle. Otherwise, the potential benefits of a global business transformation could easily be eroded by new inefficiencies.

Key process redesign activities include:

1. Mapping current processes in detail and identifying those areas that could be beneficially transferred offshore

2. Defining the future state of the organization to clearly identify the onshore/offshore interactions that will need to take place

3. Clearly defining services levels for each functional area to allow for consistent monitoring

4. Updating knowledge management systems

Sometimes process redesign involves thinking about business practices in an entirely new way. Often, that sort of innovative, outside-the-box thinking can contribute significantly to the benefits of services globalization for an organization.

Lenovo uses services globalization as an opportunity to make sure that its processes, including those that are being globalized, are done in the most efficient, effective way possible. Bandrowczak suggests posing the following question based on his former organization's experience: "As you move a function, also look at the processes that are moving and use that as an opportunity to ask: 'Can we do better?' In moving customer service quoting process to lower-cost locations, for example, we streamlined the process as we moved it."

Through these six critical steps, many companies have demonstrated successful business transformations through services globalization. What began as a purely cost-saving proposition has now proven itself as a fully transformative lever—provided that organizations use it as such.

In other words, if an organization goes into a globalization initiative with only cost savings in mind and does not take all of the six steps highlighted here, the company *may* or *may not* achieve significant cost savings, and likely *will not* see the other benefits of a full-scale business transformation.

Successful globalizers, in contrast, take on a globalization initiative with cost savings *and* other benefits—perhaps improved efficiency, increased capacity and quality of service delivery—in mind. They expect globalization to be a transformation lever for their business and they take the six steps necessary to ensure the realization of that transformative aspect.

Successful globalizers understand that, as Andrew Grove (Former CEO & Chairman of Intel) said, "A corporation is a living organism; it has to continue to shed its skin. Methods have to change. Focus has to change. Values have to change. The sum total of those changes is transformation."

Secret #2: Welcome Globalization as a Transformation Lever: Key Points

- Business transformation is one way that successful globalizers leverage services globalization to create competitive advantage.

- There are six steps to leveraging transformation opportunities in services globalization:

    - Generating solid leadership commitment. A successful business transformation—especially one as highly visible and potentially disruptive as globalization—requires the cooperation, buy-in, and commitment of an organization's employees, from the top to the bottom.

    - Developing a new organizational design and structure. Specifically, the organization must define the new roles for the global delivery centers and redefine the roles for existing centers—developing new operating models that account for new jobs and work structures, performance management systems and governance teams.

    - Collaboratively mapping out and executing change management. Here, change management involves helping existing team members to become resilient, enable knowledge transfer, engage resource planning and communicate.

    - Communicating effectively. Effective communication involves planning for the human impact of the change and identifying potential points of resistance as well as developing a plan to accommodate that impact and deal with that resistance.

    - Educating and developing new competencies. The education process should begin with the identification of training needs and development of a training curriculum for both the existing onshore and the new global organizations.

    - Redesigning business processes to include automation, new onshore/offshore interactions, knowledge management, and other support systems and to manage increasingly complex business networks. Sometimes process redesign involves thinking about business practices in an entirely new way.

- Successful globalizers expect globalization to be a transformation lever for their business.

Secret #3:

Adopt a Lifecycle Approach

.

Secret #3: Adopt a Lifecycle Approach

> Services globalization is a journey and not just a destination; it requires management of the entire lifecycle—from the knowledge phase (understanding the true services globalization opportunity) to the planning phase (developing a services globalization roadmap) and on to the sourcing and management phases.

The third secret of successful globalizers is: Adopt a lifecycle approach. Successful globalizers understand that services globalization is a journey and not just a destination. It requires management of the entire lifecycle and due diligence from the first step of understanding where services globalization fits within the business to managing offshore supplier relationships.

Where so many services globalization initiatives fail is in a lack of understanding of services globalization, in picking wrong processes and in the drop-off of oversight once a supplier is selected and the process is transferred offshore. In reality, the sourcing step is only the third in a crucial four-step process that involves knowledge, planning, sourcing and managing.

In order to successfully engage the lifecycle process, an organization must:

1. Share a belief that planning and lifecycle management is important to long-term success

2. Believe that a rigorous process, models, and data should drive decision-making

3. Develop a long-term roadmap and governance procedures to ensure adherence to the plan

Phase 1: Knowledge

The first phase of the services globalization lifecycle is knowledge. An organization must understand why it is globalizing services; understand the different supply markets; understand the different services globalization models (third-party, captive center, BOT, joint venture); and understand the risks associated with services globalization. It's been said before that ignorance is not a justifiable excuse and that knowledge is power. In services globalization, those adages are law.

The goals of the knowledge phase are to understand the services globalization opportunity and gain the knowledge that will help the organization make optimal decisions. The key tasks involved in accomplishing those goals are:

■ Conducting and/or buying market research

■ Conducting location and supplier visits

■ Understanding services globalization models

■ Understanding relevant case studies

■ Understanding peer activities

■ Understanding and internalizing best practices

■ Ensuring sponsorship of the globalization initiative at the executive level

The kind of knowledge an organization may gain in this phase of the services globalization lifecycle concerns supplier locations generally: What are the competitive advantages of each location? What are the centers of excellence? What are the risks? Sourcing to India is no longer the across-the-board best decision. The Philippines, for example, may be the optimal location for call center operations, while Russia may be optimal for high-level actuarial analysis.

An effective understanding of supplier locations will involve knowledge of exogenous factors, catalyst factors and business environments:

■ **Exogenous factors** are those that define the characteristics of the country and are beyond the influence of supplier or buyer organizations (including government support, educational system, geopolitical environment and infrastructure).

■ **Catalyst factors** are those that drive offshore service delivery in a country (including physical and time zone displacement, cultural compatibility, labor pool and language proficiency).

■ **Business environment factors** are those that relate to the direct advantages and competencies of suppliers as well as supportive business issues (including both direct and indirect cost advantages, process maturity, supplier competitiveness, supportive people factors and security/IP protection).

Also important in the knowledge phase is an understanding of the choices of ownership models: Will the company outsource to a global third-party supplier or will it build and operate its own captive center—or something in between? The ownership model decision will be affected most heavily by the company's offshore maturity and the goals the company plans to achieve with the globalization initiative.

Knowing the risks involved with services globalization is another important part of the knowledge phase. How organizations manage risk can determine the success or failure of their engagements. For example, Steve Bandrowczak says that the lifecycle approach is particularly important in that company because of the importance of reducing risk.

"We've adopted the lifecycle approach because we're trying to radically reduce our risk. We focus a lot on strategy, on being in the right markets for us, and then making sure that there's good governance to minimize risk."

Increased risk in offshoring has a number of different avoidable sources, including:

- **Minimal services globalization planning:** An adequate offshoring strategy is the key element to minimizing the risks of an offshore sourcing transaction. Yet too many companies push ahead with only minimal planning because of a perceived business necessity.

- **Limiting the scope of geographic areas:** A variety of factors work together to give a country a competitive advantage. Not understanding those unique factors and the competitive advantages of possible supplier locations can lead to a sub-optimal decision.

- **Non-comprehensive Request For Proposal (RFP):** Many RFPs focus solely on business and technology requirements instead of including offshore-specific productivity and performance-based, service-level metrics. Instead explore collaborative sourcing. Don't do RFPs says Ron Kifer, focus on collaborative sourcing and do joint solutioning.

- **Non-optimized time acceleration:** Significant loss of offshore value occurs without the right sourcing management, transition plan and engagement schedule.

- **Inadequate due diligence and supplier knowledge:** Without extensive knowledge and experience, it is difficult to do due diligence and fully understand key supplier-specific risks and capabilities. Engaging an experience third-party advisor can help organizations gain supplier knowledge rapidly.

- **Supplier-driven pricing:** Using complex contracts provided by the supplier can make comparing suppliers difficult. Use a typical market-based "offer" approach instead.

- **Inefficient negotiation**: Many negotiations focus on driving down rates without understanding the total cost of offshoring. The cheapest option is not always the best option (and may not even be the cheapest option).

- **Non-comprehensive contracting:** Not incorporating the unique terms and conditions needed for an effective contract.

▪ **Inadequate services globalization program management:** Beyond traditional oversight, specific offshore issues (including cultural and geographic issues) are often not proactively addressed.

Risk is inherent in any business decision, and no less in services globalization, but the risks highlighted above can be avoided by engaging the lifecycle methodology. Understanding the potential risks is the first step in managing them effectively.

But an organization does not have to embark on the knowledge-gaining process alone (indeed, if an organization tried it would spend years trying to get to the manage phase of the lifecycle). Instead, successful globalizers enlist established, experienced, knowledgeable third-party advisors to help educate them about supply locations and suppliers, offshore models and the risks associated with poorly planned globalization initiatives. Some of the best known firms include TPI, Equaterra, Everest and of course, Neo Advisory (Formerly neoIT).

Phase 2: Planning

The second phase of the services globalization lifecycle is planning—developing a services globalization roadmap. An organization must determine if it is ready for services globalization then determine if the process it plans to globalize is ready for globalization. The organization must also determine when each process will go global and understand, articulate and account for the total cost of offshoring.

The goal of the planning phase is to answer the questions: *Why* will the organization globalize? *Should* it globalize? *What* will it globalize? *When* will it globalize? In answering those questions, an organization creates a blueprint for its services globalization strategy. The key tasks involved in accomplishing those goals are:

▪ Assessing the global readiness of current processes within the portfolio

▪ Conducting a base-case cost analysis

▪ Defining outsourcing and globalization objectives

▪ Conducting a strategic evaluation of offshoring options

▪ Identifying candidate suppliers and locations

▪ Defining a timeframe

Why Globalize? The Total Cost of Offshoring

The first component in the planning phase of an offshoring initiative is to understand the total cost of offshoring. In the past, cost savings was for many companies the primary reason to engage in a services globalization outsourcing engagement. But now that services globalization has evolved, successful globalizers understand that global sourcing is about much more than cost savings. Global sourcing holds other benefits—including quality improvements and growth opportunities—and presents its own set of costs that, if mismanaged, could negate any potential benefits.

The total-cost-of-offshoring approach considers all of those potential benefits and potential costs and prepares the organization for managing them. The total cost of offshoring has twelve principal components:

1. Wage rate

2. Communication systems

3. Physical infrastructure and support

4. Transition

5. Governance

6. Resource redeployment

7. HR change management

8. Training and productivity

9. Disaster recovery and business continuity capabilities

10. Services globalization knowledge development/advisory services

11. Travel costs

12. Exchange rate fluctuation

Because the total cost of offshoring has eleven other components in addition to the wage rate, outsourcing processes to a low-cost supplier will not necessarily allow an organization to capture the highest value. A company can achieve maximum value by holistically evaluating an offshoring initiative in light of the organization's specific business environment.

Should the Organization Globalize? The Services Globalization Maturity Model

Even if services globalization fits well into an overall corporate strategy, many companies are not prepared to execute it. Strategically, financially, technologically and culturally, services globalization requires a certain level of preparedness that will allow the organization to work better with services globalization operations or partners and maximize return on investment. In other words, an organization must not simply assume that services globalization is a wise decision.

First, the company must analyze its services globalization maturity. Ron Kifer at Applied Materials explains, "The lifecycle is on various axes. One axis is based on the idea of globalizing the simple functions first, the more complex ones next, etc. Another axis is doing things that we know how to do—in this particular case, IT, first. BPO might be easier to do, but we don't know how to do that as an organization, so we are getting there next. What comes first, what comes next is based on maturity of the processes, maturity of the organization and sponsorship in the organization."

Looking outside itself, an organization must understand the suppliers capable of providing the services it wants to source. Global industry quality standards can help an organization do that. Standards such as the Capability Maturity Model (CMM), Six Sigma, Customer Operations Performance Center (COPC) and e-Sourcing Capability Model (eSCM) can help an organization understand the level of quality a prospective supplier could provide.

Looking within the organization is also critical. Companies need to assess their own maturity levels for services globalization in eight strategic areas, known as the Globalization Strategy framework.

Figure 4: The Globalization Strategy and Readiness Framework

Control
Ownership preference as influenced by risk and culture factors

Industry Activity
Offshore actions of competitors and industy players

Quality
Need for consistent quality

Company Culture
Affinity for outsourcing and globalization including past experiences

Globalization Strategy

Corporate Stategy
Business plan, goals and results expected acquisition, cost structure, growth, flexiblitly, risk aversion, profitabilty, cash, etc.

Cost Savings
Need for reducing cost or fundamentally altering business model

Social
Responsiblity Issues related to job loss, globalization, employee upheaval, etc

Risk
Manage stability, security, privacy, volatility, etc.

The Globalization Strategy framework is designed to help organizations analyze those specific factors for globalization readiness. Table 4 details the specific questions that an organization must ask—and answer—when determining its readiness on each factor.

Table 4: The Globalization Strategy Framework

Category	Criteria	Questions to ask
Company culture considers the organization's affinity for outsourcing and globalization, including past experiences	Change management/ international operations	Does the company have experience managing international operations?
	Infrastructure	Has enough investment and time been allocated to develop the infrastructure needed for services globalization?
Corporate strategy looks at the company's business plan, goals and results, cost structure, growth, flexibility, risk tolerance and profitability	Goals and objectives	Are globalization plans clear? Is the initiative sustainable in the long term?
	Executive champions	Does the initiative have C-level support?
	Cross-organizational buy-in	Have the necessary steps to ensure cross-divisional buy-in been taken?
Industry activity compares the offshore actions of competitors and industry players	Competition	Are globalization plans competitive with the competition?
	Industry	Are globalization plans competitive with industry standards?
Control looks at the ownership preference as influenced by risk and cultural factors	Governance framework	Is a governance framework in place?
	Audit environment	Are internal and/or independent audits of divisional processes conducted?
	Escalation procedures	Are strong, documented escalation procedures in place?

Cost savings considers the need for reducing costs or fundamentally altering the business model	Desired cost structure	Does the organization want to move from a fixed-cost to a variable-cost structure?
	Investment choice	Does the organization have a good understanding of the global ownership models and how they might be leveraged to improve the current business situation?
Quality looks at the need for consistent quality and service levels	Onshore productivity	Is the current level of process maturity high for onshore productivity?
	Offshore productivity	Is the current level of process maturity high for offshore productivity?
Risk at how a company manages stability, security, privacy, volatility, etc.	Security policies	Does the organization have a strong enterprise-wide global security policy?
	Disaster recover/ business continuity	Does the organization have an industry best-practice disaster recovery/business continuity plan in place?
	Audit environment	Does the organization conduct regular and consistent audits for process improvement and compliance?
Social responsibility considers issues related to job loss, backlash, employee upheaval, public perception and customer perception	HR policies and practices	Will we still be able to have a fair and productive workplace?
	Business ethics	Will outsourcing negatively affect the expectations of our government regulators, consumers, shareholders or other stakeholders?

What Will the Organization Globalize? Portfolio Assessment and Analysis

Sometimes even when an organization is ready for services globalization, its processes are not. The third step in the planning phase—a portfolio assessment and analysis—involves determining the readiness of the processes an organization wants to offshore.

When deciding if a particular process is suitable for globalization, an organization must consider four factors: scale, domain knowledge, maturity and complexity.

Scale refers to the size of a country's or individual supplier's operations in any given process area. When considering a supplier's scale it's important to also consider the amount of growing room that the supplier has. For example, does the supplier country's labor pool have sufficient talent for the supplier to expand its workforce?

Similar to scale, maturity refers to the amount of experience the supplier has with each process. Even suppliers with significant maturity in one process may have little maturity in another.

Domain knowledge refers to the specific expertise a supplier has in a given area. Like maturity, the length of time that a supplier has been providing a service is an important marker. But the level of service quality as well as the depth and breadth of process knowledge is critical.

Complexity refers to the level of process complexity that a supplier has experience with. Suppliers in Russia, for example, rank quite high on the complexity factor as they have a proven track record of high-quality service on complex projects. Suppliers in China, on the other hand, may possess certain strengths, but fluency in English can be a limitation.

The process that is best suited to globalization is a process that requires a high scale of activity, low complexity, a low level of domain knowledge, and for which the supplier industry is highly mature. In contrast, the process that is least suited to globalization is a process that requires a low scale of activity, high complexity, a high level of domain knowledge, and for which the supplier industry is not mature.

A portfolio assessment will help the organization determine where its processes sit on that suitability matrix. The assessment and analysis can be conducted using the following framework:

1. **Identify portfolio components:** Collect high-level data about the company's service areas to understand the nature of the business and overall internal environment.

2. **Define services globalization criteria:** Select the appropriate services globalization factors to consider when collecting, evaluating, and analyzing data from each of the service areas selected. For example, an organization with a high degree of proprietary systems will require information about IP protection and data security.

3. **Collect information:** Gather data on a variety of business function factors including total FTEs, investment required, domain knowledge required human resources factors, customer sensitivity, access/response requirement, standardization, quality, process improvement potential, and regulatory/compliance.

4. **Evaluate and score:** Use objective measures to validate information collected in step 3.

5. **Map to matrix:** Using the scores obtained from Step 4, map out what the assessment means for the ability to offshore each process.

When Will the Organization Globalize? Utilizing the Services Globalization Waves

Once an organization has answered the questions of *why* it will offshore (transformation objectives), *whether* to offshore (offshore maturity model) and *what* to offshore (portfolio analysis), the next question is *when* to offshore.

The wave strategy breaks an offshoring initiative into 30-90 day and 6 to 9 month segments that provide a definitive timeline for offshore activities to be performed and potential savings to be evaluated. In essence, the most likely candidates for offshoring will go in Wave 1, and the next likely in Wave 2, and so on. The wave strategy provides a complete schedule of what activities will go offshore and the exact timing of the transition.

Rolling out globalization initiatives in waves is critical, according to Ron Kifer, Group VP and CIO of Applied Materials. "The various components that have the potential for globalization are at varying levels of maturity and they take varying levels of time in order to put into place. In some areas it takes more time, for example, to convince the larger organization to globalize," he explains.

Former Lenovo CIO, Steve Bandrowczak, adds that it's not a one-shot deal. "It's not just one wave. Or one wave of waves. As soon as you're done with the first wave, you start all over again."

Phase 3: Sourcing

The third phase of the services globalization lifecycle is sourcing. An organization must decide the services globalization model that will work best given its services globalization maturity, the maturity of its prospective suppliers and the maturity of the process it is globalizing. The organization must consider the implications of sourcing to third-party service providers as well as the implications of building a captive center.

The goals of the sourcing phase are also to select a vendor and negotiate a contract that specifies rules of engagement. The key tasks involved in accomplishing the source phase goals are:

■   Creating requirements documents

■   Conducting a solutioning process with prospective suppliers

* Enabling suppliers to better understand the clients business

* Reviewing and evaluating each supplier's solution and proposal

* Conducting due diligence and supporting reverse due diligence

* Negotiating a contract with the right terms and conditions

Supplier selection involves four processes: visiting offshore suppliers, asking the right questions, managing service provider responses and formal due diligence. Even before due diligence, the client organization should have a good feel for: supplier capabilities, offshore models, supplier reputation, competitive landscape and geographic factors.

If an organization is sourcing to a third-party service provider, it must conduct due diligence in determining which supplier to use. Neo Advisory developed the industry's first outsourcing assurance and offshore supplier due diligence program, neoQA, which conducts quality assurance in six broad areas:

* **Financial:** Revenue growth, revenue mix, profitability, ownership and pricing.

* **Quality:** SEI/CMM certifications, ISO certification, COPC standards, Six Sigma, center-specific certifications, certification roadmaps and approach and processes.

* **Human resources:** Employee distribution, employee skills and domains, cultural fit, experience levels, recruiting and hiring, training and development, compensation and career growth, attrition management and resource utilization.

* **Client:** Services offering, clients by revenue and clients by domain.

* **Operations:** Delivery capability, sub-contracting and global distribution.

* **Infrastructure:** Physical infrastructure, IT infrastructure, disaster recovery and business continuity.

Due diligence should also uncover the breadth and depth of a supplier's domain knowledge, project and program management skills, customer and partner satisfaction, management skills (including geography, project size, project type, and experience), transition process and management, and flexibility (including comfort level and experience in various pricing models and service agreements).

In addition to due diligence, the sourcing process also involves price negotiations and contract writing. A comprehensive contract will cover:

- Deal structure

- Risk management

- Price structure and protection

- Quality assurance

- Change management

- Personnel management

- Core resources

- Exit clauses

- Transition details

- Termination clauses

- Core resources

- Knowledge transfer

- IP protection and access

- Regulatory and legal issues

- Governance

For successful globalizers, the sourcing phase is not just about selecting a supplier. "For FedEx, it's about flexible global resourcing—how you integrate flexible capacity from the supply-side or the offshore operations into your organization," says FedEx's CIO, Rob Carter.

Phase 4: Manage

The fourth phase of the services globalization lifecycle is management. This is a phase that is applicable to not just post-contract but plays a role in strategy and sourcing too. While each lifecycle stage is critical, most services globalization engagements fail not because they were improperly sourced or planned but because they were improperly managed.

The goals of the management phase include: 1) providing ongoing contract governance; 2) providing ongoing program management; 3) ensuring that performance is in line with quality expectations; and 4) realizing the strategy and projected benefits. The key tasks involved in accomplishing those goals are:

- Determining the performance impact of the transition

- Defining and implementing processes for issue and risk management

- Effecting transition

- Managing performance, relationships, contracts, resources and finances

- Conducting a health check

The governance framework establishes six key management areas within a services globalization governance plan:

1. **Resource management**: Retention, training, vacations, holidays, resource transitions, knowledge transfer and skills updates.

2. **Performance management**: Service levels monitoring and reporting, schedule management, quality control issues, offshore workload management and process flow for onsite and offshore delivery.

3. **Financial management**: Invoice review, expense allocation, invoicing procedure and change management to base model.

4. **Contract management**: Key personnel, staffing, attrition, background checks, insurance, disaster recovery and business continuity plans, and reformulating service levels for relevancy.

5. **Relationship management**: Initiative choices, teamwork, tracking issues to closure and bridging culture gaps.

6. **Risk management**: Risks should be identified within all of the above five areas and tracked and mitigated. These should also address monitoring of external factors.

The management phase of the services globalization lifecycle begins with transition management, which involves six steps from the beginning of the engagement to complete hand-off. Those steps are:

1. Transition planning and key resource retention

2. Change and cultural management

3. Risk assessment, impact analysis, asset protection and mitigation plan

4. Knowledge transfer

5. Reengineering of work flow

6. Reaching steady state

Another aspect of effective governance is risk management. Risk management should cover the following areas:

- Business continuity and disaster recovery

- Customer privacy

- Information protection

- Insurance coverage

- Intellectual property rights

- Network security

- Personnel security

- Physical security

Establishing a services globalization program management office is one key way to maintain governance over the engagement. In addition, an annual health check is key to the maintenance and continual improvement of the offshore engagement. That check should cover such issues as evaluation of service levels, updated benchmarking, productivity and pricing versus the market, and adherence to industry best practices.

Successful globalizers also realize that the knowledge, plan, manage and source phases of the lifecycle are not discrete, one-off projects. As Ron Kifer, Group VP and CIO at Applied Materials explains, "One important aspect of the lifecycle approach to globalization is the idea that the core competency of today is the contextual activity of tomorrow. So we're constantly evaluating our internal organization and deciding over time what is still core, what is still value-added, what still provides a competitive differentiation and refocus our resources on that and move those things that have evolved and matured into contextual activities to our managed services partners. And we know that's a continual, evolving process, and you have to have a model that recognizes that and accommodates for it."

A unique model being leveraged by Applied Materials is the partnering of a number of supply management functions to Neo Group. While Applied Materials leaders continue to own governance, Neo Group team members manage day to day resource management, performance management, contract management and process discipline management.

Case Study: Fortune 500 Retailer Fails at Numerous Offshore Attempts Before Adopting Lifecycle Approach

A Fortune 500 retailer wanted to reassess its IT services and develop a global resource model to help the company retain its current competitive advantage and build capacity. The company's pilot, however, had faced internal resistance, long project delays, cost overruns and poor internal customer satisfaction.

We found that the retailer didn't understand the difference between offshoring and outsourcing (knowledge), didn't make an optimal decision on what to offshore (planning), didn't make an optimal decision on where to offshore (sourcing) and had no governance framework at all (managing). Our goal was to capture the current status of the engagement, identify performance gaps and the root cause of the time delay, and propose recommendations for moving forward.

To begin, we conducted a detailed assessment of 5 major IT application groups. Based on the outcome, we developed a high-level transition strategy that provided the retailer with a tentative application roadmap. Through the use of frameworks, we were able to guide the retailer's core team through a process that allowed for the identification of the application groups appropriate for migration and for the development of a resource plan for the identified applications. We merged this information with the inputs gathered from key stakeholders to develop vendor evaluation criteria, comparison, and ranking.

We also helped the retailer develop a transition roadmap for the applications identified as suitable for globalization. The roadmap consisted of a comprehensive and realistic set of guidelines and plans to effectively transition the in-scope applications.

Throughout this process, Neo Advisory engaged to jointly create a governance model and structure that would enable the retailer to manage its global offshoring projects effectively. The governance framework included defined roles and responsibilities and information processes to prevent the recurrence of cost overruns and missed timelines.

After we had worked with the retailer through the knowledge, planning, sourcing and managing steps of the lifecycle, the client began to realize its projected gains from the offshoring initiative.

Adopting a lifecycle approach to services globalization is one of the most critical behaviors of successful globalizers. Through knowledge, planning, sourcing and governance, successful globalizers mitigate the risks involved in their initiatives and maximize the benefits.

If offshore outsourcing was ever a simple decision of moving IT processes to India and business processes to the Philippines, services globalization is now a complex decision that involves the consideration of multiple service locations and suppliers as well as the analysis of a full range of business processes, including core functions.

Though complex, services globalization need not be overwhelming. By following the processes outlined here, and enlisting the help of an experienced sourcing consultant, an organization can make the best global sourcing decision.

Secret #3: Adopt a Lifecycle Approach: Key Points

- Adopting a lifecycle approach to services globalization is one of the most critical behaviors of successful globalizers.

- The lifecycle approach requires due diligence from the first step of understanding where services globalization fits within the business to managing offshore supplier relationships.

- The first phase of the services globalization lifecycle is developing knowledge— understanding the true services globalization opportunity:

  - The goal of the knowledge phase is to gain an understanding of why the organization is globalizing services; the different supply markets, services globalization models and risks associated with services globalization.

  - The key tasks involved in the knowledge phase include conducting market research, visiting locations and suppliers, understanding services globalization models, understanding relevant case studies, understanding peers; understanding and internalizing best practices and ensuring sponsorship of the globalization initiative at the executive level. Successful globalizers often enlist the help of third-party advisors to accomplish those tasks.

- The second phase of the services globalization lifecycle is planning— developing a services globalization roadmap:

  - The goal of the planning phase is to answer the questions: *Why* will the organization globalize? *Should* it globalize? *What* will it globalize? *When* will it globalize?

  - The key tasks involved in the planning phase are: Assessing the global readiness of current processes within the portfolio, conducting a base-case cost analysis, defining objectives, conducting a strategic evaluation of sourcing options, identifying candidate suppliers and locations, and defining a timeframe.

- The third phase of the services globalization lifecycle is sourcing:

  - The goals of the sourcing phase are to select a vendor and negotiate a contract that specifies rules of engagement.

  - The key tasks involved in the sourcing phase are: Creating requirement documents, joint solutioning, collaborative sourcing, reviewing and scoring each supplier's solution, conducting due diligence and negotiating a contract.

- The fourth phase of the services globalization lifecycle is managing:

  - The goals of the management phase include: Providing ongoing contract governance and ongoing program management, ensuring that performance is in line with quality expectations and realizing the strategy and projected benefits.

  - The key tasks involved in the management phase are: Determining the performance impact of the transition, defining and implementing processes for issue and risk management, effecting transition, managing performance, relationships, contracts, resources and finances, and conducting periodic health checks. Each services globalization engagement must be managed as if it were the organization's first.

Secret #4:

Align Business and Globalization Objectives

Secret #4: Align Business and Globalization Objectives

> It's true that any company that wishes to survive in today's global market must adopt a services globalization strategy. But not every company is ready to globalize *every* process *today*. Instead of blindly jumping on the services globalization bandwagon, successful globalizers look at globalization in relation to their overall business strategy. They ask: Is our business strategy driving our services globalization strategy? What part of our business strategy does globalization help us execute?

I've said before that a company that wishes to flourish in today's global market must adopt a services globalization strategy. But not every company is ready to globalize *every* process *today*. A successful services globalization strategy takes diligent planning and thought—and that takes time and focused effort.

In the last chapter on adopting a lifecycle approach (Secret #3), we talked about answering the following questions: *Should* the organization globalize? *Why* will the organization globalize? *What* will the organization globalize? *When* will it globalize?

The last two questions are more operational than strategic; the first two—about why the organization is globalizing and if it even should globalize, are purely strategic. In answering those strategic questions, an organization must look at globalization in relation to its overall business strategy. If the two don't align, the organization is wasting its resources and should not globalize.

When talking about GE's globalization strategies, former CEO Jack Welch, arguably one of the best strategists of modern business and a highly successful globalizer, says "If GE's strategy of investment in China is wrong, it represents a loss of a billion dollars, perhaps a couple of billion dollars. If it is right, it is the future of this company for the next century."

Not every organization will risk billions of dollars in its globalization strategy, but each runs the risk of unsuccessfully globalizing and missing out on the opportunity to complement business strategy with globalization. In order to successfully leverage services globalization—to "be right" in globalization decisions—organizations must ensure that their globalization strategy is driven by and aligned with their business strategy.

The sections that follow aim to offer insight into the questions an organization needs to ask when determining if its business strategy and globalization strategy align.

Is business strategy driving services globalization? What part of your business strategy does globalization help you execute?

Ensuring That Business Strategy Drives Globalization Strategy, Not the Other Way Around

As services globalization becomes a business imperative for industries from financial services to health care, companies will be even more inclined to jump on the bandwagon with their peers. Afraid of being left in the dust, too many companies globalize without really considering whether services globalization is right for them—and whether their particular approach to services globalization is the best one.

While it's true that services globalization is becoming a business imperative and should receive due consideration from executives at every organization, services globalization is not a one-size-fits-all proposition: the way Company A executes its global strategy will not necessarily work for Company B, just as the reasons for Company B to globalize are not necessarily the same as Company A's reasons.

In other words, too often globalization initiatives are taken on with no real strategy at all. Or an organization allows its globalization strategy to drive its business strategy. Successful globalizers, in contrast, develop very clear globalization strategies before setting one foot out the door, and those plans are driven every step of the way by the corporate strategy.

Applied Materials' Group VP and CIO Ron Kifer says that aligning business and globalization objectives is really about securing the future for the company. "Your business strategy should be the primary driver of the globalization strategy because globalization doesn't happen in isolation. If you look at what Applied Materials is doing with globalization, we're all-around optimizing performance and focusing on the core, critical competencies of the organization, the cost-effectiveness of the solutions closer to our customers, and that means a different geographic footprint."

Successful globalizers thoroughly assess their business process portfolio, financial state, goals, objectives, risk and transformation needs, as well as the supplier landscape and market capabilities in provider locations. Using information from those assessments (which are detailed in Table 1), successful globalizers build a globalization strategy that includes the following elements:

- Future proofing

- Risk management

- IP protection

- Transformation

- Service extension

- Resource redeployment

- Innovation management

Armed with a globalization strategy, successful globalizers develop an execution roadmap, which includes:

- Geographic placement

- Ownership model

- Third-party supplier relationships

- Transition timing

- Financial return

- Governance organization

Case Study: Too Much, Too Fast

One S&P 100 global investment bank offers a good example of a company that did not allow its business strategy to drive its globalization strategy. Instead, perhaps eager to jump on the bandwagon of financial services firms adopting services globalization, the company globalized too much, too fast.

The organization globalized its application development, application support and maintenance, IT infrastructure management, and internal IT help desk all at the same time. Overloaded and lacking a clearly defined globalization strategy, the investment bank began to experience performance and quality issues with its offshore internal IT help desk services.

To remedy the problem, the organization had to backtrack, taking steps that it would have been wiser to take initially, including securing buy-in from key client stakeholders, providing for effective knowledge transfer, and building a well-planned, solid governance framework. After taking those steps and determining that its newly defined services globalization strategy did follow its overall business strategy, the company was able to successfully resume its initiative.

Having a Clear Idea of the Part of the Business Strategy That Globalization Will Help Execute

In addition to aligning its globalization strategy with its business strategy and ensuring that it is the business strategy that's the driver, the successful globalizer has a clear idea of what part of its business strategy globalization will help execute.

Former Lenovo CIO Steve Bandrowczak explains that globalization is not just for the sake of lowering costs. "We were lowering costs not because we were not competitive in the industry. We were lowering costs because our stakeholders expected it and competition demands it. You keep getting back to what are the strategic objectives of your business."

Bandrowczak added that in his staff meetings, the alignment between globalization and business strategy was crystal clear. "If you had sat in my staff meeting, we didn't say 'Okay we're going to shut two data centers down and we're going to save three centers.' Instead, we said 'We're going to improve our expense-to-revenue ratio from an IT perspective because we're going to get in line with industry standards and we have to deliver $100 million to the bottom line of Lenovo.' You constantly have to keep tying your global initiatives to those business and strategic directions."

Case Study: Lack of Clarity and Definition

A Fortune 500 electronics company provides an example of an organization that did not develop a clear idea of the part of its business strategy that globalization would help execute before beginning its globalization initiative. As a result, the organization encountered a number of (avoidable) problems.

The company initially decided to offshore its corporate business customer service, retail customer service, levels 1, 2 and 3 customer support, order processing, accounts payable and receivable, and order-to-cash processes to third-party suppliers as well as a captive center in India and the Philippines.

Once the initiative was underway, the electronics company found significant performance and quality issues with corporate business customer service processes within its captive center. Additionally, the ramp-up of higher-end, customer-facing processes was slower than the company had originally expected.

After analyzing the problems that had occurred within its services globalization initiative, the organization realized that its fault lay in not fully analyzing its portfolio of processes to understand the fundamental what, when, where and how questions that services globalization requires. Additionally, the company found that its fragmented processes needed to be aggregated and that an effective transition needed to be based on a detailed analysis of processes.

This Fortune 500 electronics company responded to the deficiencies it found in its services globalization rollout, re-planned the initiatives by answering those critical what, when, where and how questions, and developed a clear picture of how globalization would help the company accomplish its business objectives. Now it has very successful offshore operations.

Case Study: Leading with Strategy

A Fortune 500 health and life insurance company provides a good example of the strategic considerations a company might make at different levels of the organization. This company had a very fragmented and inefficient life claims process, with no existing manuals or desktop procedures. Each examiner had his or her own version of the process and method for calculating claim amounts.

In addition, the organization was bogged down in paper-based calculations that were full of errors with no audit trail. Furthermore, process output/productivity, accuracy, and efficiency were not tracked. As a result, the firm was unable to leverage its systems and knowledge to compete in the market against new players.

This organization resisted the urge to adopt services globalization as a fix-it solution to its inefficiencies. Instead, it considered its strategic goals and how it could accomplish those goals with an aligned services globalization strategy. Each executive team member contributed in a different way to the strategic development: the CEO had a strategic focus, concerned with leading the business into the future; the CIO took a performance focus, concerned with flexibility, productivity, guaranteed services levels and proven technology. The CFO took a bottom-line focus, concerned with reducing current costs and managing future costs.

Instead of using services globalization as a substitute for sound business strategy, this Fortune 500 health and life insurance company used a well-developed services globalization strategy to complement its business strategy, which was geared in part toward overcoming several process inefficiencies.

Secret #4: Align Business and Globalization Objectives: Key Points

- Not every company is ready to globalize every process today. A successful services globalization strategy takes diligent planning and thought—and that takes time and focused effort.

- An organization must look at globalization in relation to its overall business strategy. If the two don't align, the organization is wasting its resources and should not globalize.

- When determining if its business and globalization strategies align, the organization must ask two questions:

    - Is business strategy driving services globalization? Successful globalizers develop very clear globalization strategies through thorough assessments of their business process portfolio, financial state, goals, objectives, risk and transformation needs, as well as the supplier landscape and market capabilities in provider locations.

    - What part of the organization's business strategy does globalization help execute? In addition to aligning its globalization strategy with its business strategy and ensuring that it is the business strategy that's the driver, the successful globalizer has a clear idea of what part of its business strategy globalization will help execute.

Secret #5:

Assign the Best People

Secret #5: Assign the Best People

All too often, organizations simply use the most easily accessible people to guide globalization initiatives, even when those people are not right for the job. In many of those cases, the initiatives don't reach their full potential. Successful globalizers, in contrast, select the "best people"—people who are resilient, embrace change, have global mindsets and affinities for different cultures, are performance-oriented, take initiative, are admired by others within the company and are consensus builders. With the best people at the helm, the globalization initiatives can find strong support at all levels of the organization.

Globalization is not about a single action, or even a group of actions. Globalization, when successful, is about an attitude. Yet even when the CEO of a company embraces globalization as a new attitude, it will fail unless their partners—the people who work for them—embrace the attitude as well. But getting others on board is not a job the CEO can do alone; they must recruit the best people to help.

That's what the fifth secret is about: recruiting the best people to help roll out (and guide) globalization initiatives throughout the company. With the best people at the helm, the globalization initiatives can find strong support at all levels of the organization.

Wim Elfrink, Chief Globalization Officer of Cisco says that assigning the best people was a key success factor for the company. "Assigning the best people is a key differentiator between what we did differently from companies that traditionally approach the management of outsourcing. We had to have the right people empowered as decision-makers on both sides of the house. We insisted on having people who could make the decision in the actual negotiation process. And that was huge in us being able to accelerate the timeline and deliver value. I don't think that you can afford to do anything else in this process."

From finding out what on-site employees really care about to making visits to supplier locations, these six retention strategies will help minimize the number of times that one of your best employees catches you in the hall and asks "Do you have a minute?" (Too often, that conversation ends with the employee walking out the company's door—and that costs the company a lot.)

Assigning the best people to their globalization initiative just makes sense for successful globalizers. "Our philosophy is: you put your best people on the project and it's successful. You take your second- or third-level people and put them on the initiative, and you're going to get a second- or third-rate result. Globalization deserves the organization's best people. It's a top-priority project within the company," said Ron Kifer, CIO at Applied Materials.

As football great Vince Lombardi said, "Individual commitment to a group effort is what makes a team work, a company work, a society work, a civilization work." The fifth secret of successful globalizers is about generating that individual commitment to the group effort.

Strong participation from the organization's C-level executives is important for its role-modeling effects and to help generate buy-in within the organization's lower levels.

In addition, attention and recognition by senior management make it easier to lure the best talent to lead globalization initiatives. And developing the practice of strategic learning will allow the organization to take advantage of the myriad of opportunities our increasingly interconnected world offers.

This secret reminds me of the adage, "You get what you pay for." If the organization doesn't put its best people in charge of services globalization—if it sends in the B-team, for example, it will see second-rate results.

The "Best People"

The best people are not necessarily those who know the most about IT, if the organization is globalizing IT, for example. Instead, they're the people who are agile, understand change and are globally savvy. All too often, companies trade the sometimes challenging task of finding the best people in favor of the most easily accessible people, even when those people are not right for the job. In many of those cases, the initiative does not reach its full potential.

When former GE CEO Jack Welch was globalizing the company in the 1980s, his best people were those who knew how to adapt to, and even embraced, change. He defined the best people not as the best performers, but as the best fit for a globalized, cross-cultural environment.

Consider a common example of what can happen when an organization doesn't assign the best people: The company decides to globalize its IT processes, so it assigns the IT managers to lead the initiative.

Those IT managers are extremely well-versed in IT processes and have a lot of knowledge about the company's IT system, but are overall more reserved, introverted types. They shy away from high-profile leadership roles and generally dislike change.

The organization thinks that the IT managers can guide the initiative because they know IT, in spite of their shortcomings as globally savvy leaders. Yet the initiative falls short.

Why? While the IT managers played an important role in the organization's IT department, they were not often the best people to lead a globalization initiative. They lacked most of the important "global people" characteristics. The "global people" stars are resilient, embrace change, have a global mindset and an affinity for different cultures, are performance-oriented, take initiative, are admired by others within the company and build consensus.

Take another example of an organization that assigns a number of leaders from different departments within the organization. These people have a record of embracing—even spearheading—change. They seek out high-profile roles and enjoy leading others; they're admired and have proven their ability to build consensus among employees.

Despite the fact that most of these people know little about the day-to-day details of the organization's IT processes, the organization assigns them to head the initiative. The initiative succeeds.

Why? The organization assigned as leaders those people who had demonstrated the ability to be good leaders and possessed many of the "global people" characteristics. When they needed to understand the details of IT processes, they sought out the IT managers, who were able to do what they did best.

Indeed, being one of the company's "best people" is not necessarily about knowing things, Wim Elfrink of Cisco explains that it's more about the right business relationships. "It's not about knowing the scope of definition of the activities from the start; that's all detail to be added. Instead, we looked for people who understood proper contextual relationship that we were going to establish with these service providers—people who understood the business relationship and could make obligations to that business relationship."

While not many people embody all of the "best people" characteristics, putting together a team that conjointly possesses all the qualities is one of the key secrets of successful globalizers. The following table details the "best people" characteristics and why they're important in a globalization initiative.

Table 1: "Best People" Characteristics

The best people. . .	Because. . .
Are resilient	No matter how good the team of people assigned to lead the globalization initiative, it will likely be met with resistance. The best people are able to stand firm against that resistance, stay focused on the message and retain their belief that the change is necessary for the health of the company.
Embrace change	Change is an opportunity for renewal; the best people understand that and relish change for every opportunity it may offer.

Have a global mindset	They understand the interconnectedness of our world and respect the business necessity of globalization.
Have an affinity for different cultures	They respect different cultures and understand that other cultures, economies, and countries offer a host of new business opportunities.
Are performance-oriented	They are those who measure success by performance. They focus on the individual's contribution to the team and the team's performance as a whole. They prefer to focus on the act of doing and the outcome.
Take initiative	They feel empowered to make decisions; they're go-getters. They've made taking initiative in a variety of different situations a habit.
Are admired by others within in the company	They are leaders who others love to follow. People know who they are and admire them.
Are consensus builders	They demonstrate an understanding of the importance of consensus in a globalization initiative and they have proven abilities to build consensus, even in controversial situations.

At Cisco, Chief Globalization Officer, Wim Elfrink looks for people who have "a never-ending desire to be challenged and to win. "I think that it's a special A-type personality who absolutely enjoys driving these big changes. I always say that at the end of the day, the best people want to leave their mark. Their mark is the big change—the big results that they deliver. I think you'll find that consistent with people who are good at globalization—they really do enjoy it."

The Importance of C-Level Participation

Even with the "best people" leading the globalization initiative, the importance of executive-level buy-in and participation can hardly be understated. If the organization's leaders won't wholeheartedly commit to globalization, lower-levels employees can't be expected to, either.

While the "best people" are not necessarily at the C-level, strong participation from the executives is still important. A 2003 Best Practices in Managing Change survey by Prosci found that the top five changes respondents would make in their organizations' communication approach included more communication from executive sponsors and senior managers. The survey reaffirms that employees do look to their executives for broad-based guidance and role modeling.

Wim Elfrink states it this way: "Get C-level commitment up front and engage the people who can actually make the appropriate decisions in the process. Then empower the initiative leaders. You don't want those lower-level people taking every pertinent discussion a level up in the organization."

One important aspect of the CEO's job in the initiative is to communicate with the organization. At Plantronics, for example, CEO Ken Kannappan uses a communication tool called "Gold Mail." "It's a tiny little thing but it's really working well for us. We send out frequent short e-mails, which are PowerPoint slides together with audio recording that goes with the slides. It allows me, in all languages around the world, to say something with the slides so that everyone globally can understand what's going on."

The Importance of Strategic Learning

The organization that wishes to be a successful globalizer must necessarily become what author Peter Senge calls a "learning organization"—one that "is continually expanding its capacity to create its future."[1] Perhaps the greatest opportunity that globalization offers companies is the ability to do just that—to create their future.

Globalization has opened up a whole new world of possibilities. But to simply rely on old paradigms to take advantage of those possibilities would be to miss out on the greatest potential of globalization. The learning organization, instead, will each day consider throwing out yesterday's paradigms and creating new ones that more aptly describe the world as it is today and, consequently, today's new business opportunities.

To become a learning organization, according to Senge, enterprises must adopt the fifth discipline, "systems thinking." Systems thinking is about seeing the world as a series of connected events which each play an important role in the fate of the whole. Looking only at individual events without considering the whole system is to miss the point altogether.

That's especially relevant for today's global organization. As organizations, economies, cultures and people become increasingly connected, an ability to comprehend our individual effects on the whole system becomes increasingly important. No longer do our behaviors only affect a small circle of connected people and organizations—often, our behaviors today send ripple effects around the world.

Senge says that "the prevailing system of management is, at its core, dedicated to mediocrity... It forces people to work harder and harder to compensate for failing to tap the spirit and collective intelligence that characterizes working together at their best."[2] Successful globalizers create their own systems that are dedicated to excellence.

---

1   Senge 14.

2   Peter M. Senge, The Fifth Discipline: The Art and Practice of the Learning Organization (New York: Doubleday, 2006) xviii.

Globally-Savvy Leaders

Even with the best people on board, C-level participation, good communication and a commitment to strategic learning, managing in a global services environment is a complex job that requires a special kind of manager—a globally-savvy one. There are certain key competencies that are required to succeed as a global manager and certain key qualities that globally savvy managers have in common.

Adaptability

Globally savvy managers don't just cope, they adapt. Surveys have demonstrated that the inability to manage change is one of the most significant barriers to a successful global sourcing initiative. So a globally savvy manager will not only know how to manage change, but how to communicate the benefits of that change to the appropriate decision-makers.

Global Mindset

Globally savvy managers have a broadened mindset. They can look across situations, business segments, and cultures and focus on the commonalities rather than the differences. They think globally when considering business opportunities.

Global Sourcing Experience

One characteristic most globally savvy leaders share is experience. Steve Bandrowczak, Lenovo's former CIO, calls that experience "stripes on his back." "First and foremost, being a globally-savvy leader starts with having gone through services globalization and having the capabilities—I call it stripes on my back. Of course, where you learn a lot, you make a lot of mistakes. One of the things you start to get is a feeling for how you navigate around these pitfalls, how you tell when the organization isn't ready for the change, how you find good people, all those things that are more instinctive—that you can't turn to a textbook to read." On the other hand, many companies are adopting the Certified Outsourcing Professional (COP) training and recognition awarded by the International Association of Outsourcing Professionals (IAOP) to help their team members gain global sourcing experience faster. This is a program that is not just text book but rewards experience and engages the learner in a rich case study based learning style.

Another characteristic that Bandrowczak sees in globally savvy leaders is the ability to create what he calls a burning platform. "At Lenovo, we had 24 months from the day I started to roll out SAP across 66 countries to get 5,000 IT systems on the IBM side. So how do you do that when most companies take five years? We created a burning platform. I said 'After May, 2008, if I'm not off the IBM infrastructure, it costs me $11 million per month in penalties.'"

"So when someone on the team wanted to talk about whether to use a UNIX system or an NT system, this version of SAP or another, a blue screen or a red screen, I say 'No problem, if you're going to add 30 days to the program, just show me the $11 million.' With that burning platform, I could drive these changes because a three-month slippage in our world was thirty-three million dollars, and that's close to half of the gross profit at Lenovo at that point in time."

Cultural Agility

Globally savvy managers have the ability to lead well across different cultures. They're most often strong leaders who have an affinity for adjusting well to unfamiliar situations. They understand that cultural differences are complex and have the potential to derail a sourcing initiative.

Some organizations look to managers from the sourcing location for their understanding of the complexities of working globally, knowledge of the local cultural landscape and network of strong relationships in the sourcing location (for example, the client may hire a Filipino living and working in the U.S. as the global manager for an offshoring initiative to the Philippines).

Or the client may hire an American manager who has experience as an expatriate for her knowledge of the U.S. business culture and global experience as an expatriate. Ideally, client organizations will blend the two approaches, says Lori Blackman, Founder and President of human capital consulting firm DNL Global.

Strong Relationship Management and Communication Skills

Globally savvy managers are not only good at managing relationships across business segments and cultures, but they also know key individuals within the organization. Globally savvy managers establish and maintain active networks and strong relationships through the following skill sets:

Strong Performance Management Skills

Globally savvy managers can engage and motivate their employees—even those who are thousands of miles away. They also understand how to develop local talent—instead of relying on more expensive and sometimes less effective expatriates.

Finding and/or Developing Globally-Savvy Managers

Because traditional managers may not have the skills necessary to become excellent global managers, some organizations resort to poaching globally savvy managers from their competitors. But that's not a viable long-term solution. To succeed globally in the long-term, client organizations need to learn how to find and/or develop their own globally savvy managers.

Some globally savvy managers seem like they were just born that way—they're out there for the organization to find. Finding them is about knowing the indicators of a globally savvy manager—understanding the qualities that they possess.

But globally savvy managers can also be developed from within the organization. Key steps to developing them include:

Creating Global Learning Opportunities

Developing programs that offer managers the opportunity to work outside the organization's home country—through expatriate programs or temporary assignments abroad—can be a first step in developing the adaptability and cultural agility that are so important in a global sourcing manager.

But bi-cultural expatriate and temporary work-abroad assignments may not help managers develop the necessary global mindset. To foster that development, organizations should work to create global teams—to internationalize their ranks. That can allow for global learning opportunities on both the institutional and the individual levels.

Building a Global Leadership Factory

Organizations should invest from the top down in programs to create global leaders. Global leadership factories can be semi-formal internal programs or formal educational opportunities outside the company.

Corporate education programs are great places for managers to develop global leadership abilities—picking up relevant skills and learning from others' experiences. The programs are also great places to build networks and absorb global culture and values.

From knowing how to identify a globally savvy manager to how to develop one, the ability to create a global leadership team with the qualities of the globally savvy manager is essential to the success of any global sourcing initiative. As important as other aspects of talent management are in their own right, the client needs a globally savvy manager to lead the initiative to success.

As I shared before, leverage programs such as the COP certification from IAOP and other training programs available on Global Ability to augment your team's skills.

The HR Perspective on Assigning the Best People

From the HR perspective, assigning the best people to head up globalization initiatives involves four activities: recruiting, performance management, development and rewards.

Recruiting

Talent management has been in the news lately as employers in the U.S. and other developed economies face a shortage of skilled workers—a shortage that will only grow as the Baby Boomers retire from the workforce. In this environment, attracting and retaining top talent has become a fundamental key to remaining or becoming a competitive business.

How, then, can organizations recruit talent? They could—and often do—fight over the scarce talent that's available onshore. But that may not be the most efficient or effective option.

Looking globally to find talent—and sourcing work to where the talent is located—can be a great alternative to engaging in a talent war. Many global companies may already be globalizing to take advantage of offshore talent pools; in the 2006 Duke CIBER/Booz Allen offshoring study, almost 70% of respondents reported that offshoring is driven by a desire to tap the global talent pool.[3]

Steps to Developing a Successful Global Recruiting Model

Recruiting offshore can be quite different than recruiting onshore. There are cultural barriers to be overcome, brand recognition to be established, compensation structures to be understood. But taking the four steps necessary to accomplish these and other tasks can pay off in the form of access to pools of highly educated, competent employees.

Step1: Identify talent needs

Before going global to recruit talent, it's important that the client organization identify the particular skills and capabilities that it needs. Does the company need call-center employees, back-office payroll processors or software engineers to design and implement a web-based self-serve benefits site?

Step 2: Assess Sourcing Options

Once talent needs have been identified, the organization can ask the right questions about potential sourcing options. Assessing the options with regard to the organization's particular needs and goals is important; the organization should specifically consider each location's competency in the area(s) in which talent is needed.

When considering potential sourcing locations, assess what works and what doesn't in the offshore markets being evaluated. Analyze data such as labor costs (including unique compensation structures and trends), tax implications, unionization and benefits liabilities, as well as people issues such as cultural compatibility, community impact and employee engagement. Understand the general and location-specific cultural and other risks that can results from offshoring.

---

3   2006 Duke CIBER/Booz Allen offshoring study, The Globalization of White-Collar Work. Available at http://www.boozallen.com/publications/article/16945601?lpid=66005

Step 3: Devise a Proactive Talent Strategy

In today's talent-short environment, a proactive recruiting strategy is essential. It's not enough to place a want ad and hope that successful candidates apply—your competitors are proactively recruiting the successful candidates while you wait. Job portals such as bestoutsourcingjobs.com can help but one needs more.

To develop a proactive talent strategy, reach into multiple sourcing channels. Consider hiring a recruitment process outsourcing (RPO) firm or other trusted advisor with experience in the specific channels you're considering.

Talented candidates across the globe can now afford not only to be picky about which companies they work for, but they can also be more demanding. Many talented employees report that they highly value learning and development opportunities within their companies. So the organization should commit to developing training programs. Help employees prepare long-term development plans and match those plans with existing work opportunities.

Step 4: Engage the Offshore Model with a Focus on Organizational and People Issues

Recruiting offshore can be made more difficult by a local unfamiliarity with the company brand. So when entering offshore markets to recruit talent, companies need to develop an employment brand and advertise it to potential recruits.

Genpact, for example, set up "storefronts" in eight Indian cities out of which employees can recruit local talent. Candidates can walk in and chat with company representatives about what Genpact does and the kinds of opportunities it offers; they can leave their resumes; and then they can come back later for voice and accent testing, when necessary.

Keep in mind that the most lucrative talent pools may be in Tier-II cities. In many of these locations, potential employees will need to be sold not only on the company, but on BPO or ITO itself as a career. Recruiters should highlight the wide scope of BPO as a career as well as the company's opportunities for advancement.

Once the purview of companies that wanted to reduce costs or leverage growth opportunities, services globalization now counts among its drivers the need to get talent where it's located—which is increasingly offshore. Global sourcing requires companies to develop a global recruiting model; companies that can successfully do that may be able to stay ahead of the looming talent wars.

Performance Management

Those who embody the "best people" characteristics will likely already be performance-driven and oriented toward high achievement. They will also likely appreciate the thought that their leadership in the globalization initiative may be a way to rise to the top of the organization. But even for the best people, and especially for others, managing performance—ensuring that set goals are met and new goals are set—is an important part of keeping the organization moving toward globalization.

In addition to measuring performance, it's often important to motivate and provide incentives to employees to meet or exceed their goals. Part of performance management, then, is delivering rewards for high-level performance as well as consequences for low-level performance. It must be made clear to employees that just as helping the company achieve success in globalization will pay off in rewards; hindering the company's success (or simply not helping) will generate adverse consequences.

Development

In some cases it's acceptable to develop people who are not the best people into the best people and allow them to run the globalization initiative. For example, many companies facing a lack of qualified leaders in IT, for example, choose not to find the best people within other facets of the organization to lead the IT globalization, but instead choose to develop the "best-people" characteristics of those IT managers who also possessed the technical knowledge necessary to successfully globalize the IT processes.

Retention

The effects of competition for global talent will filter through a company's retention strategies, too. In a high-demand environment, organizations must work even harder to keep their employees from being drawn away by other firms. There are a number of steps that client organizations can take to mitigate the attrition problem both on-site in their own organizations as well as offshore in the supplier organization.

Key Steps to Reducing Attrition in the Retained Onshore Team

Step 1: Find Out What Employees Care About (Hint: It May Not Be All About Financial Rewards.)

Too often, employers assume that employees care predominantly about their compensation. It's true that compensation is important. But employees often care as much, or more, about non-financial aspects of their jobs.

When an organization wants to find out what matters to its employees, it should ask. A heat map is one way to gauge employees' levels of job satisfaction and to understand what the employees care about. It's a periodic survey that asks employees about their levels of job satisfaction in a number of areas—from job roles and responsibilities to career development and growth opportunities, engagement experience and compensation. A quick and meaningful response to the heat map results is the key to making heat maps an effective retention tool.

Step 2: Develop a Mentoring Program

Mentoring is one important way that organizations can build employees' affinity for the firm. Different from coaching, mentoring is a strategic endeavor that provides a forum for the mentored to develop professionally and personally. Benefits for the mentored include:

- Access to the mentor's expertise and experience

- Skills development

- Broader view of the firm

- Exposure and visibility

Step 3: Develop a Culture Which Encourages Engagement

Engaging workers so that they feel they've positively impacted the company's performance is a prime retention tool that's equally important onshore and offshore. A Towers Perrin study revealed that 59% of workers who consider themselves engaged intend to stay with their employer, while only 24% of workers who consider themselves disengaged plan to stay.[4] Engagement drivers are often those same factors that employees care about—from opportunities for career growth to feeling proud of the organization.

Step 5: Create Incentives

Providing behavioral incentives—even for already highly self-motivated people—can be a quick way to success. Jack Welch, one of the first and most successful globalization leaders, told me that during his time as the head of GE, he met weekly with his team of best people, to not only ensure that they were working on the same goals as he was, but to also offer them incentives as needed to help motivate their progress. In many cases, that incentive may be the opportunity to rise in the organization.

At FedEx, providing incentives to encourage the best people is not about tangible rewards. Instead, the company has developed an overall atmosphere of support and encouragement. "We call our philosophy the 'Purple Promise,'" Rob Carter says. "It's all about people, boundaries and work encompassing the entire team. We make sure to focus on people so that they can take the responsibility we ask them to. We help them to understand how their participation makes things better for the whole company. We say to our employees: 'Our promise is to put you first.'"

---

4   Towers Perrin, Winning Strategies for a Global Workforce. Available at www.tower-sperrin.com/tp/getwebcachedoc?webc=HRS/USA/2006/200602/GWS.pdf

Key Steps to Reducing Attrition in the New Offshore Team

Step 1: Work With Suppliers to Manage Retention

Working with suppliers to manage retention in offshore third-party arrangements involves a number of efforts, including:

- Looking closely at prospective suppliers' retention levels and policies for managing the factors that lead to attrition during due diligence

- Holding suppliers accountable by building attrition metrics into Service Level Agreements (SLAs)

- Encourage the supplier to develop non-poaching agreements with other suppliers

- Ensure that the supplier addresses high stress levels, which are a leading cause of attrition in offshore BPO and ITO firms

Step 2: Design Rotational Exchange Programs

Exchange programs that let key offshore employees work onshore at the client site for 3 to 6 months help those employees feel a greater level of affinity for the client organization as well as a greater sense of engagement. Also, an exchange program gives employees the opportunity to learn about the client organization's culture, method of operation, and products and services—knowledge that the employee can bring back to the supplier organization to help boost performance. Make similar opportunities available to your employees.

Step 3: Show Your Face

Providing quality face time with key members of the client organization is a critical way to build cultural affinity for the client, facilitate growth in important personal relationships, boost loyalty and encourage engagement. One way to show your face is to make regular visits (perhaps quarterly) to the supplier location. But there are other, less costly ways as well; personal phone calls are effective as a more frequent way of "showing your face" as well. Ron Kifer leverages Cisco's TelePresence product very effectively to stay in touch with his teams and leaders.

Secret #5: Assign the Best People: Key Points

- All too often, companies simply use the most easily accessible people to guide globalization, even when those people are not right for the job. In many of those cases, the initiatives fail.

- The "best people" to guide a globalization initiative are resilient, embrace change, have a global mindset, an affinity for different cultures, are performance-oriented, take initiative, are admired by others within the company, and build consensus.

- While not many people embody all of the "best-people" characteristics, putting together a team that conjointly possesses all the qualities is one of the key secrets of successful globalizers.

- From the HR perspective, assigning the best people to head up globalization initiatives involves four activities:

  - Recruiting. While it's better to assign the best people from within, recruiting may play an important role in assigning the best people.

  - Performance management, which ensures that set goals are met and new goals are set, and is an important part of keeping the organization moving toward globalization.

  - Development. In some cases it's acceptable to develop people who are not the best people into the best people and allowing them to run the globalization initiative.

  - Retention. Behavioral incentives—even for already highly self-motivated people—can be a quick way to success.

- The importance of executive-level buy-in and participation can hardly be understated. For if the leaders won't wholeheartedly commit to globalization, lower-levels employees can't be expected to, either.

- Developing the practice of strategic learning will allow the organization to take advantage of the myriad of opportunities our increasingly interconnected world offers.

Secret #6:

Implement a Strong Governance Model

Secret #6: Implement a Strong Governance Model

A strong governance model will help guard against the most common problems that plague services globalization initiatives post-rollout. It can help an organization maintain post-contract executive focus, no matter what changes occur at the C-level; monitor key performance indicators and ensure that deliverables are in line with expectations; and keep the original goals and contractual terms at the fore and modifying them when business changes require it.

When I make presentations at client conferences, I often ask this question: What is the single largest factor contributing to the failure of services globalization initiatives?

The answers I receive range from "lack of good project managers", "supplier incompetence" to "miscommunication" to "internal resistance." But in my experience, a great percentage of services globalization initiatives fail because of the client organization's inadequate attention to governance.

What is Governance and Why is it Important?

Secret #3 (on adopting a lifecycle approach) covered management as the fourth phase in the services globalization lifecycle. Governance is an integral part of that phase. And, just as management of the initiative is as important during the knowledge-gathering phase as it is during steady state, so is governance equally important throughout the various stages of the services globalization initiative.

Governance usually gets a lot of attention during the rollout period of the initiative. It's after steady state has been reached and executives have moved on to new initiatives that governance often gets forgotten—though it's as important during steady state as it is any other time. The most common problems that I've seen plague services globalization initiatives post-rollout include a lack of executive focus after the contract has been signed, insufficient monitoring of performance and deliverables, contract amnesia and a loss of original objectives.

A Lack of Executive Focus After the Contract's Been Signed

Whether the executive team has moved on to a new business initiative, the company has experienced a changing-of-the-guard at the executive level, or the company has moved to pursue new business drivers, I often see globalization initiatives drop off the executive agenda once rollout is complete.

Insufficient Monitoring of Performance and Deliverables

In the 1978 Superman movie, Christopher Reeve's Superman catches Lois Lane mid-fall and says, "Easy Miss, I've got you."

"You've got me?" Lois exclaims, "Who's got you?!"

The question can be all-too-familiar in business, as everyone assumes that someone else has assumed responsibility.

But in a services globalization initiative, a lack of direct monitoring of performance and deliverables can lead to reduced quality and missed or misaligned expectations. Even if a client organization is monitoring service levels, there are other performance criteria such as attrition levels that are critical to the continued success of the initiative. Without direct monitoring, the quality of service may suffer.

Contract Amnesia

Even when service providers do not intentionally move away from the terms of a contract, a lack of continuous enforcement leads to complacency, and often leads to a creeping away from the terms of the contract. On the other hand, in a business environment as fluid as today's, circumstances, needs and goals often change mid-initiative. Without an institutionalized means for making sure that the contract follows those changes, the contract loses relevance.

Loss of Original Objectives

Just as changing objectives can lead to contract amnesia, they can also lead to the loss of the original objectives; the goals that launched the services globalization initiative in the first place. As the lifecycle of a globalization initiative progresses, changing objectives are natural—flexibility is one quality that most successful globalizers share.

A strong governance model can maintain post-contract executive focus, no matter what changes occur at the C-level; it will monitor a number of key performance indicators in addition to service levels and ensure that deliverables are in line with expectations, and it will keep the original goals and contractual terms at the fore, modifying them when business changes require it.

Three Layers of Governance

The successful governance model, shown in Figure 5, operates on three levels: the organizational level, the functional level and the operational level.

Figure 5: Governance Across the Organization

Organizational Governance

The top tier in the pyramid reflects organizational governance. At this level, governance activities are primarily strategic and are engaged by the organization's senior leaders. Organizational governance is where the big picture is reconciled, where the firm's business case for globalization is aligned with the initiative itself. This level of governance focuses on achievement of strategic objectives through services globalization and monitors that progress.

Lenovo's former CIO Steve Bandrowczak describes how governance was structured at the organizational level there:

> "You've got to make services globalization a business project and you've got to make it where the business leaders of all impacted functions are either on the steering committee or part of the regular executive update program.

> In the transformation program at Lenovo, every two weeks the CEO and his direct reports would be on a one-hour conference call going through the exact details about what decisions had been made, where they were on the rollout and how they were doing against the benchmarks.

> So at least we had all decisions not only cleared off the table but communicated and there was a running list of all the key stakeholders that needed to be made a decision that were potentially holding up a program as well as the actual status and budget against the project.

With these kinds of real and critical projects, people are involved at an extremely high executive level. Everyone puts in time and owns these programs. A lot of times you hear of executive sponsorship that only really involves giving senior executives quick updates every six months. But that's not ownership.

The worst thing you can do is make your globalization initiative an 'IT program.' Even if it's just a data center, it still impacts your business. You've got to have the program where it's business-owned and business-led, and you've got to get the business to buy in."

Functional Governance

At the functional level, governance activities are more hands-on than at the organizational level, but less than at the operational level. Here, the role of the governance group is to enable coordination, communication and control among key stakeholders and functional leads. Focus is on functional synergies and coordination rather than day-to-day management.

Operational Governance

The operational level is the front line of an initiative's governance activities. This is where individual contracts and relationships are managed. The operational governance team is responsible for monitoring the day-to-day activities within the initiative as well as for reporting from-the-ground information to the functional and organizational governance teams.

Because the operational governance team is directly responsible for managing the initiative on a day-to-day basis, large organizations may have several operational governance groups in place across divisions or functional areas.

Plantronics doesn't think of global services governance any differently than it thinks of traditional business governance. "It's no different here than it is anywhere else. So it's really kind of what our overall governance and management model is," CEO of Plantronics, Ken Kannappan explains.

"As a practical matter, most decisions are made as far down in the organization as we can push them. We try to limit the number of large meetings we have—unless they're really focused on best practices or something like that, because it just tends to clog everybody's time and schedule."

Key Components of the Governance Operating Model: The M5 Framework

Within a governance model that spans the organizational, functional and operational layers of the organization there are five key management areas. Neo Advisory developed the M5 framework to define those areas, which cover performance management, financial management, contract management, relationship management, and resource management.

Table 5 details the key activities involved in each of the five management areas as well as their benefits.

Table 5: Key Components of the Governance Operating Model

	Activities	Benefits
Performance management	▪ Analyze trends in service lines (SLs) ▪ Reorganize work process flow for offshore delivery ▪ Monitor continuous performance improvement efforts ▪ Review workload distribution across resources ▪ Recommend productivity enhancements ▪ Perform monthly operations reviews	▪ Early indications of problems ▪ Forecast of shift scheduling ▪ Maintain focus on quality improvements ▪ Consistent performance levels ▪ Optimal utilization of resources ▪ Implementation of global delivery model
Financial management	▪ Facilitate renegotiation of pricing model when triggered by volumes ▪ Validate one-time expense allocations ▪ Help modify pricing model for moving up the value chain	▪ Value for money, quality, flexibility ▪ Industry benchmarking of market rates ▪ Proper utilization of allotted one-time costs ▪ Improved global sourcing
Contract management	▪ Track adherence to SLs ▪ Redefine SLs for relevance ▪ Review DR/BC planning and testing ▪ Review compliance with insurance requirements ▪ Review HIPAA compliance and data security ▪ Track volume levels for pricing model triggers ▪ Monitor sufficiency of connectivity/infrastructure	▪ Contract compliance ▪ Ensuring SLs are a true reflection of vendor performance ▪ Recommend new SLs for raising the bar ▪ Ensure planning for 24/7/365 operations ▪ Mitigate regulatory risk ▪ Achieve next level of economy of scale globalization ▪ Ensure offshore center availability

Relationship management	▪ Maintain vendor's focus on client as "Client of Choice" ▪ Ensure continuity of clear organization escalation path on both sides ▪ Track issue logs and days to closure ▪ Clear up any cultural miscommunications ▪ Facilitate offshore-onsite interactions	▪ Vendor remains involved in engagement at the executive level ▪ Avoid issue accumulation due to executive-level changes ▪ Early issue resolution ▪ Seamless integration between client and supplier ▪ "One Team" atmosphere
Resource management	▪ Review resource profiles for recruitment ▪ Monitor on-boarding processes ▪ Ensure smooth transition of key resources ▪ Review attrition figures and retention strategies ▪ Monitor skills/new process training ▪ Assist in employee recognition	▪ Right resource for the right job ▪ Early on-the-job productivity ▪ Attrition management ▪ Project continuity ▪ Process-specific, not people-specific delivery ▪ Knowledge management is built for future transitions, if any ▪ Prepare offshore for growth and moving up the value chain ▪ Increase individual productivity ▪ Generate loyalty to the engagement

Performance Management

If the organization has practiced its due diligence in the knowledge-gathering, planning and rollout phases, it can be relatively comfortable that the supplier's performance will meet expectations. But even when the highest level of due diligence has been practiced, even when the client organization has a history with the supplier, performance must still be monitored, recorded and managed.

Performance management will be much more effective during the governance phase if internal processes have been well documented during the knowledge-transfer and rollout phases. By documenting how processes are best completed in-house, the client organization will have a benchmark against which supplier performance can be measured. Without reliable benchmarks, performance management will only create confusion and breed discontent between the client and supplier organizations.

At FedEx, tracking performance is a hallmark of the company's success. "Make sure you have a great tracking system," Rob Carter, FedEx CIO told me. "At FedEx, we use that data to make sure we understand the variability in our business and to solve problems and to continuously improve the business."

Leading firms are using tools like Oblicore, Enlighta, Digital Fuel or Janeeva to report service levels and create enhanced transparency.

Financial Management

Even as organizations look to services globalization to realize a number of benefits, improving the bottom line by reducing costs is still often a key motivator behind global sourcing initiatives. Financial management, then, is critical as initiative stakeholders will be watching the financial case closely throughout the engagement.

Even where a contract is airtight and due diligence has been executed to the highest level, unexpected costs inevitably arise. The purpose of financial management, then, is to monitor, record and manage those costs to ensure that they don't end up negating the company's original financial case for globalization and thereby derailing the initiative.

An understanding of the client organization's financial pressures—as well as a perceptive knowledge of the supplier's resource management strategies—can create a methodical and efficient framework for managing unbudgeted expenses, including resource transitions, vacation and cultural holiday coverage strategies, unallocated travel costs, resource training needs and turnover costs. The global program manager, whose purpose is to bridge the gap between the supplier and the client, should be well positioned to manage these financial challenges.

Contract Management

The globalization lifecycle discussed in Secret #3 detailed the source phase and how an important part of that phase is the contract writing. But for all the attention that needs to be paid in the contract writing and negotiating phases, compliance with the carefully laid-out contract terms must be monitored. Just as performance management is important even with the most high quality, competent suppliers, monitoring contract compliance is important even with the most by-the-books suppliers.

Enforcing contract compliance with periodic reviews will preempt issues relating to questions about responsibility, work processes, performance and delivery. In the worst case, inadequate, inconsistent contract enforcement can lead to business discontinuities that can't be adequately addressed because lines of responsibility are unclear and accountability is hazy. In the best case, inadequate, inconsistent contract enforcement does not cause business discontinuities that adversely affect the customer, but will at the least create tension in the client-supplier relationship over where responsibility lies and who is ultimately accountable for what.

In contrast, rigorous monitoring and consistent contract enforcement may prevent damaging business discontinuities and will at least nurture a healthy partnership between the client and the supplier with both parties having consistent views of their contractual obligations.

Relationship Management

Most successful businesses understand the importance of relationship management, between company representatives and customers, between upper-level and lower-level managers, and between managers and their direct employees. But relationship management is often more difficult within a services globalization initiative as cultural differences arise between client and supplier organizations.

Cultural differences are one important reason why a successful governance model includes a global program manager who is located in the supplier country and understands the culture there. As key players in the client and supplier organizations get to know each other, the global program manager plays the important role of cultural liaison, facilitating people-related issues, communicating across cultures and providing a conduit for the exchange of information and ideas.

Resource Management

Managing resources within a globalization initiative requires more structure and rigor than most organizations are accustomed to. It is essential that the people assigned to each job have the right domain knowledge, prior transitioning experience and good communication skills. The importance of resource management is more critical among the initiative leaders and governance managers. The difficulty arises as these important tasks are transferred to an entirely new set of people, often in a culturally different, far-away location.

The Program Governance Office

The lack of a single, unified management office is a leading cause of initiative failure, says Ron Kifer, Group VP and CIO at Applied Materials. "More often than not, the reason these managed service initiatives fail is because there is no single point of contact for the engagement—for vendor negotiations, for vendor management, for contract management."

Ultimately, it is the Program Governance Office (PGO) that is accountable for the ongoing success of the services globalization initiative. That doesn't mean that the PGO has to bear the weight of governance at all three layers; instead, it means that the PGO is where the proverbial buck stops.

"The PGO is key to long-term success. Certainly it's key in negotiations. You can't have every business leader in the negotiation—there has to be a single point of contact throughout the entire process and then a single management entity with responsibility across the whole enterprise, because globalization is not just about IT—it's an enterprise solution," Kifer explains.

The PGO bears the ultimate responsibility for ensuring that good governance is being practiced within all three layers. A successful PGO will do that by:

1. Ensuring that accountable resources are identified for individual program management and execution (expectations should be clearly outlined as well as the consequences of failing to meet responsibilities).

2. Ensuring that schedules and plans are synchronized for all project constituents.

3. Ensuring that Client Business and Operations groups are linked and synchronized.

4. Ensuring executive sponsorship, user acceptance and buy-in throughout the engagement.

While the Project Governance Office is a part of the client organization, a successful program manager will assign a dedicated on-site manager (a global project manager) to act as a liaison between the client and the supplier organizations.

The global project manager may be a direct employee of the client organization who relocates to the supplier country (the do-it-yourself model); an employee of the supplier's; or an independent local third-party oversight organization. Applied Materials leverages Neo Group to help it manage, monitor and improve IT supply relationships.

Table 2 details the requirements, advantages and disadvantages associated with each type of global program manager model.

Table 2: The Global Project Manager Model

	Requirements	Advantages	Disadvantages
Do-it-yourself	▪ Client manager (expatriate) needs to have deep insight into the onsite/ offshore delivery model	▪ Effective for scale ▪ Allows client organization to retain more control	▪ Client manager will take time to develop an understanding of local supplier practices ▪ Culture gaps will be an issue ▪ If the client manager quits, the client will have to start all over again ▪ Least cost effective (the average cost to the client including travel, relocation, etc. is $500,000 per year)
Rely solely on supplier	▪ Rely on supplier reporting ▪ Rely on supplier world view ▪ Tighter contract compliance mechanism		▪ Multiple suppliers means multiple views ▪ Supplier has a vested commercial interest in playing down the severity of problems ▪ Loss of control

| Use a local independent third party | ▪ Third party should have knowledge of local delivery practices ▪ Third party should have experience in globalization best practices ▪ Third party should have domain knowledge of client business processes ▪ Should represent client organization's interests ▪ Should be supplier-neutral | ▪ Local presence ▪ Can act as a cultural bridge ▪ Most cost-effective solution ▪ Third-party organization will ensure backup and continuity even during periods of turnover | |

In most cases I recommend that client organizations use an independent third-party oversight organization that is in the same location as the supplier to act as the global program manager. I never recommend that a client organization rely solely on the supplier for governance, and the do-it-yourself model is usually only effective when a client organization has a large presence in the location already and can leverage economies of scale.

Whichever global program manager model is chosen, the best global program manager will understand the cultural and business climate in the supplier country and have experience working with client and supplier organizations in global arrangements. Specifically, a successful global program manager will have direct experience with and knowledge of supplier methodologies as well as an understanding of the client's business processes.

Table 3 details the activities that a successful global program manager will undertake in each governance area.

Table 3: The Global Program Manager's Governance Activities

Governance area	Activities
Performance management	▪ Evolve a robust workflow and process for both organizations ▪ Focus on service levels in the contract that have a direct bearing on success ▪ Focus on gap-closing processes
Financial management	▪ Manage financial expectations in the contracting phase ▪ Prepare the client organization and supplier to expand their global engagement into other areas of the business ▪ Create awareness about unbudgeted expenses such as resource transitions, turnover, cultural holidays, etc.
Contract management	▪ Set up consistent compliance meetings as a regular checkpoint for deliverables, unresolved issues, and service level monitoring ▪ Apply the terms of the contract from the beginning ▪ Monitor adherence to contract terms
Relationship management	▪ Hand pick the user/IT staff that forms the core team from those who have a positive stake in the success of the globalization initiative ▪ Build trust, relationships and effective partnerships over time ▪ Secure and check executive sponsorship throughout the organization ▪ Pro-actively manage issues so that they do not snowball ▪ Communicate regularly, especially during periods of transition
Resource management	▪ Specify those key personnel in supplier organization who cannot be reassigned without prior client approval ▪ Prescribe a 10% resource buffer ▪ Allow 2 to 3 weeks of overlap to transition resources ▪ Agree on a process for the movement of personnel ▪ Oversee investment in both technical and process training and management and professional training

Case Study: Using Governance to Solve a Business Problem

A Fortune 500 financial services firm provides a good example of how an organization can resolve a global business problem through good governance. The firm's business challenges included:

- Large size and number of different stakeholders. The firm's retail banking division alone has four separate lines of multi-billion dollar business. The firm found that each division's distinct objectives, cultures and levels of profitability hurt the organization overall.

- Multiple suppliers. The organization had multiple third-party vendors in a variety of geographic locations as well as captive centers providing business support.

- Issues of cost, non-standardized services, and management control.

- The migration of a large number of resources.

- Consistency across the organization. The firm sought to ensure that all initiatives within and across its divisions could be executed in a predictable and repeatable manner and lessons learned could be shared across the organization.

The organization's first step toward a solution was recognizing that there was a problem—that operations needed to be synchronized worldwide and common measurement, evaluation and escalation processes had to be created.

The second step was more difficult: figuring out how to create the solution— consistent, confluent operations and management—in such a large, diverse organization. Fortunately, the firm had some operational governance structures in place; the task was to deploy those governance frameworks throughout the organization.

The organization-wide governance framework involved actively managing the external and internal service providers through Neo Advisory's M5 framework as well as clearly defining the roles and responsibilities of all key players within the organization.

In creating that organization-wide governance framework, the firm put in place program monitoring and issue escalation process standards and—at the same time—created a complete program management framework to use for its current and future globalization initiatives.

Good Governance Shows

Will Whitehorn, President of Virgin Galactic and a member of Virgin's inner circle, says that although Virgin has more than 200 companies, there has never been a major fraud committed there. He attributes that success to a very strong governance structure. "We have governance through ownership of the brand name, through equity ownership, and because we put some management into each business."

One member of Virgin's fabled "Group of 8"—the organization's investment committee which includes the most senior members of the company—Whitehorn sits on the Board of every one of Virgin's largest businesses. The Group of 8 ensures that those companies are practicing good governance.

Implementing governance across the organizational, functional and operational layers of the business, managing each governance area and setting up a global program management office are all critical steps in establishing a strong governance model. But successful governance requires more: It requires accountability and responsibility; a strongly staffed governance team and an investment of time, effort and money.

In terms of financial investment, successful globalizers usually spend 5–8% of their overall initiative expenditure on governance. The financial investment that will be required to fund a successful global governance program will depend on a number of unique factors.

Governance team members at the operational level should expect to spend approximately 12–28% of their time and effort on governing globalization initiative. Executive-level team members should expect to spend about 5% of their time and effort on governance. Of course, the time and effort that each team member expends on governance will depend on the stage of the initiative, its complexity, the relationship between the client and the supplier, and the prevailing roles within the client organization.

One of the difficulties in outsourcing—whether local or global in nature—is the loss of control. While a project management office is critical and the client organization has a right to exercise a certain amount of control over supplier resources and processes, ultimately the control is in the supplier's hands.

And while control and accountability are not one in the same, a loss of control may mean a loss of accountability. The client organization will have to work diligently to maintain a clear line of accountability within its own organization and between itself and the supplier. Ultimately, it is the project management office that is accountable for the success of the initiative, though the PGO will certainly transfer a large number of responsibilities to other key parties.

The organizations that already have a strongly defined and enforced accountability and responsibility structure will clearly find that aspect of the services globalization initiative much easier than companies that do not have those structures in place. But even companies that are not accustomed to defining accountability can learn to do so and engage a successful globalization initiative.

In the end, the purpose of governance is to ensure that the goals set out for a services globalization initiative are being met. An organization may embrace globalization (Secret #1), welcome it as a transformation lever (Secret #2), adopt a lifecycle approach (Secret #3), align business and globalization objectives (Secret #4), and assign the best people (Secret #5), but if the organization walks away from the initiative at that point, it may fail.

Establishing a strong governance model helps to ensure that globalization continues to be embraced and welcomed as a transformation lever; that the lifecycle is followed through; that business and globalization objectives are consistently re-measured and realigned; and that the best people stay on the job. It is only with strong governance that an organization can secure the continued success of its globalization initiative.

Secret #6: Implement a Strong Governance Model: Key Points

- A strong governance model will help guard against the most common problems that plague services globalization initiatives post-rollout. It can maintain post-contract executive focus, no matter what changes occur at the C-level; it will monitor a number of key performance indicators in addition to service levels and ensure that deliverables are in line with expectations; and it will keep the original goals and contractual terms at the fore, modifying them when business changes require it.

- The successful governance model operates on three levels:

    - The organizational level, where governance activities are primarily strategic and are engaged by the organization's senior leaders.

    - The functional level, where the role of the governance group is to enable coordination, communication and control among key stakeholders and functional leads.

    - The operational level. The operational governance team is responsible for monitoring the day-to-day activities within the initiative as well as for reporting from-the-ground information to the functional and organizational governance teams.

- Within a governance model that spans the organizational, functional, and operational layers of the organization there are five key management areas: Performance management, financial management, contract management, relationship management and resource management.

- Ultimately, it is the Program Governance Office (PGO) that is accountable for the ongoing success of the services globalization initiative.

- The successful program manager will assign a dedicated on-site manager (a global project manager) to act as a liaison between the client and the supplier organizations. That global project manager should understand the cultural and business climate in the supplier country and have experience working with client and supplier organizations in global arrangements.

- Successful governance requires accountability and responsibility; a strongly staffed governance team; and an investment of time, effort and money.

Secret #7:

Embrace a Continuous Improvement Mindset

Secret #7: Embrace a Continuous Improvement Mindset

> Embracing a continuous improvement mindset throughout the lifecycle of the global initiative allows successful globalizers to understand how well the initiative is working. As a part of that mindset, successful globalizers conduct regular health checks at the following points: prior to completion of the sourcing phase, post-transition, midway through the initiative, and at contract-renewal time.

Many client organizations undertake global sourcing initiatives without an accurate understanding of the management that will have to be involved for the initiative to be successful. That's why the sixth secret is to implement a strong governance model. But how will the client organization know if its governance model is strong enough? If its global sourcing initiative is successful? That's where a continuous improvement mindset comes in. Embracing a continuous improvement mindset throughout the entire lifecycle of your sourcing initiative will allow you to understand how well the initiative is working.

Plantronics CEO Ken Kannappan explains that the company spends at least 10–20% of its time on continuous improvement. "If you go to our factory, 10% of time there is spent on improving operations. We spend a huge amount of time on this. In R&D, 20% of time is spent on process improvement."

There are a number of well-thought-out, tested models for process improvement. Six Sigma has proven the most resilient as well as, importantly, the most cross applicable throughout a variety of different kinds of processes in a variety of different kinds of industries.

Six Sigma: Seeing the Forest *and* the Trees

One of Six Sigma's contributions to global sourcing improvement comes from its focus on processes. Six Sigma's forefather, Dr. W. Edwards Deming, cautioned to "Eliminate slogans, exhortations and targets asking for zero defects or new levels of productivity. Such exhortations only create adversarial relationships, as the bulk of the causes of low quality and low productivity belong to the system and thus lie beyond the power of the workforce."

Deming spent much of his career promoting what he called his "85/15 rule"—that 85% of productivity problems were built into the system and only 15% of the problems were the fault of individual employees. To fix productivity problems, then, the organization must focus on the system—on the processes.

In Secret #2, on welcoming globalization as a transformation lever, talks about leveraging globalization to improve processes. But if processes are flawed because of the institutionalized way of doing things within the organization, simply shipping a few back-office processes overseas may not solve the problem. That confounds many executives, who expect globalization to be a panacea. But Six Sigma teaches us that to improve our business we must look at the cause of the problem, and fix the cause—not just the problem.

That means, according to George, Rowlands and Kastle[5], that "if you want to improve quality, you have to change the way work is done."[6] To do that, George, Rowlands and Kastle say, "You need to become a process thinker—someone who frames problems and issues in terms of what may be happening in the process. Making this mental leap has a much more profound effect than it may sound at first."[7]

I'm reminded of a story author Peter Senge tells in his book, *The Fifth Discipline*, about a man who fell into a river at the base of a dam. No matter how he struggled against it, the man could not swim out of the back flowing current at the dam's base. He died of hypothermia. After he died, the current sucked his body underwater, where it was caught by the downstream current and eventually surfaced about 10 yards downstream. If the man had dived down below the back flowing current—instead of futilely struggling against it—he would have been carried downstream where he could have been rescued.[8]

The tragic story, Senge writes, is an example of "structures of which we are unaware [that] hold us prisoner. Conversely, learning to see the structures within which we operate begins a process of freeing ourselves from previously unseen forces and ultimately mastering the ability to work with them and change them."[9]

Listening to the Voice of the Customer

Another of the great contributions we take from Six Sigma is its focus on the voice of the customer (VOC). As George, Rowlands and Kastle describe, "The companies who will do best in the marketplace are those who take the time to see everything through their customers' eyes and deliver what they want."[10] If your product or service isn't what your customers want, it's defective. The ultimate goal of Six Sigma is to eliminate defects.

Of course, the definition of "customer" can vary. Is your customer external—those who purchase and use your products and services? Or is your customer internal? Or perhaps your primary customers are shareholders. No matter who you serve

5   Authors: Mike George, Dave Rowlands and Bill Kastle, What is Lean Six Sigma?
6   Mike George, Dave Rowlands and Bill Kastle, <u>What is Lean Six Sigma?</u> (New York: McGraw-Hill, 2004) 20.
7   George, Rowlands and Kastle, 28.
8   Peter M. Senge, <u>The Fifth Discipline: The Art and Practice of the Learning Organization</u> (New York: Doubleday, 2006) 92.
9   Senge, 93.
10   George, Rowlands and Kastle, 12.

most directly, say George, Rowlands and Kastle, external customers "are ultimately judges of your company's products or services. They're the ones who determine whether or not your company will be profitable."[11] So even if you're in the Finance department, you're ultimately responsible for your company's external customers as much as the customer service representatives are.

In that respect, understanding the voice of the customer ties into the fourth secret of successful globalizers: Align business and globalization objectives. Sourcing payroll processes to the Philippines may be en vogue, but if it doesn't ultimately help you serve your customers better, you shouldn't be doing it.

DMAIC

Carpenters often repeat the dictum, "Measure twice, cut once." In global sourcing, a wrong cut doesn't have to be the end-all—most mistakes can be fixed, but it is often more tasking to fix them once they've already come up than to preempt them. That's ultimately what Six Sigma is about—not fixing problems once they come up ("putting out fires") but understanding the fundamental flaws in processes so that problems can be eliminated before they ever arise.

To do that, client organizations should institutionalize Six Sigma's preeminent improvement model: DMAIC. DMAIC, an acronym for **D**efine, **M**easure, **A**nalyze, **I**mprove and **C**ontrol, is a step-by-step way to institutionalize the concept of continuous improvement. Indeed, a continuous improvement mindset is like a record player that plays DMAIC over and over. It's DMAIC in every process, every engagement and every stage. By continuously defining, measuring and analyzing, the client organization can continuously improve (and maintain those improvements).

Define: Making the Business Case

In Six Sigma, the define stage is about agreeing what the project is: What is the process that will be improved? Why does it need to be improved? What will the organization gain by improving the process? How will success be measured?

As it applies to services globalization, the define stage is about determining your globalization objectives. Recall Secret #4, align business and globalization objectives, which asserted the importance of defining globalization objectives that are in line with the organization's overall business objectives.

Measure: Creating Internal Benchmarks to Measure the Success of the Initiative

Measurement really defines what Six Sigma is about. It separates Six Sigma process transformations from ad-hoc projects with results that are short-lived and/or disappointing. George, Rowlands and Kastle write about the measure

---

11   George, Rowlands and Kastle, 13.

stage of DMAIC: "Combining data with knowledge and experience is what separates true improvement from just tinkering with a process."[12]

This stage is particularly important in services globalization, especially with its tendency that many organizations have to simply rush off and outsource a process to China without really considering the reasons behind the move, planning for its success or defining how success will be measured.

Chapter 3 discusses the measurement stage, calling it the knowledge phase of the globalization lifecycle approach. Recall that the knowledge phase involves the following key tasks:

* Market research

* Supplier/location visits

* Understanding services globalization models

* Understanding relevant case studies

* Understanding peers

* Understanding and internalizing best practices

* Ensuring sponsorship of the globalization initiative at the executive level

Knowledge gathering, or measurement, is about more than investigating sourcing suppliers and locations. It's also about looking deep into your organization's processes and understanding how you will set the stage for improvement through services globalization.

Applied CIO Ron Kifer says that measurement is a critical factor in his company. "In this respect, a global sourcing initiative is no different from any large change program," he explains. "If you don't have before metrics and you don't know what your end target metrics are going to be, you'll never know whether you've improved or not improved."

At Lenovo, for example, cycle time from order to delivery was extremely important. As the company centralized many of its global supply chain functions, it had to work hard to continuously improve its order-to-delivery times. The key, Bandrowczak states, was "getting metrics around your cycle times and those key drivers for your business—making sure you had those before-and-after and then constantly challenging yourself on how to improve those metrics."

Lenovo also developed internal benchmarks that it used to foster continuous improvement across the business. Bandrowczak continues:

---

12   George, Rowlands and Kastle, 63.

"As we rolled out infrastructure and systems and solutions in a country, we were benchmarking that country against another. We did India and then had China up and running; we had about 40% of our shipments and revenue running through our global system. We were benchmarking China against India across all processes. Then what we did was to take those benchmarks and forward project them against other countries. So, for example, how many people would it take to process $5 million of invoices or X number of receivables or X number of payroll transactions—whatever those key metrics were, now that you had a benchmark in terms of those processes, these systems, you should be able to forward project. So you say 'If I take these processes and these systems and implement them in France, for example, it takes 3 people in India, it takes 16 people in France today, if I forward project, I better make sure I get down to 3 people in France if it has a similar type of volumes and business.'

One of the things that happens—and it happens very, very often—is that as you roll out new systems and infrastructure, you were supposed to do it with 3 people now all of a sudden you have 16 people who are busy. Of course they're going to be busy if they haven't benchmarked it against anything and you haven't said 'Hey I can do this with 3 people in country Y, why is it taking 16?' Then you start to benchmark against the two

countries and what you'll find is a lot of non-value added, a lot of wasted energy."

Analyze: Planning for the Initiative by Gathering Knowledge

The analyze stage encompasses taking the data that's been gathered in the measure stage and making sense of it. George, Rowlands and Kastle caution that "A challenge that all teams face in Analyze is sticking to the data, and not just using their own experience and opinions to reach conclusions about the root causes of problems."[13]

Analyze is the first stage in which the vision of process improvement really begins to come into focus. It's akin to the plan phase discussed in Secret #3, on the lifecycle approach, where you'll develop a globalization roadmap for your organization. Recall that the tasks you'll tackle in the plan/analyze phase include:

- Assessing the feasibility of globalizing current processes within the portfolio
- Conducting a base-case cost analysis
- Defining objectives

---

13   George, Rowlands and Kastle, 67.

- Conducting a strategic evaluation of offshoring options
- Identifying candidate suppliers and locations
- Defining a timeframe

Improve: Putting the Sourcing Engagement to Test

In Six Sigma, the improve stage is where the proverbial rubber hits the road. It's in this stage that all of the data gathered, measured and analyzed in the previous stages gets put to work to make process changes to eliminate defects. This is the source stage from Secret #3, which details the lifecycle approach. The tasks required in this stage include:

- Creating requirement documents
- Conducting a scripted walk-through with prospective suppliers
- Conducting joint solutioning
- Reviewing and scoring each supplier's solution
- Conducting due diligence
- Negotiating contract

In the improve/source stage it's important to stay focused on the process improvement plan you created in the analyze/plan stage. Otherwise you run the risk of creating solutions that don't really solve the core problems you identified, or coming up with solutions that have proved ineffective in the past.

Control: Managing the Engagement

The last phase of the Six Sigma DMAIC model is control, managing the realized improvements. In this stage, you'll want to take steps to ensure that the improvements you've made through the last stages will last. To do that, George, Rowlands and Kastle suggest:

- Documenting the new, improved procedures
- Training everyone
- Setting up procedures for tracking key "vital signs"
- Handing off ongoing management of the process

- Completing the project documentation—creating your globalization playbook[14]

In Secret #3 and #6, we talk about managing the sourcing relationship and implementing a strong governance model. While it may seem counterintuitive to those who are globalizing services for the first time, it is critical to continuously govern the initiative—even with the best suppliers, continued governance is critical to ensuring that the improvements last.

Many companies look at global sourcing as merely a cost-cutting proposition. While it certainly is that, it is also so much more. Successful globalizers understand that managing sourcing engagements over time isn't just about continuous cost improvements, but about overall quality improvements as well.

Ron Kifer, Group VP and CIO Applied Materials, states that his focus is on quality improvements over "wringing costs out perpetually over time." He says, "What we really want to do is maintain a very market-competitive price point with our service provider, but we're most focused on service improvement, on quality improvement, on business agility and time to market. These are the things that we're looking for and that we built into our contract as far as what to expect for continuous improvement in the model that we put in place—not necessarily a focus on continuing to take year after year after year of cost reduction."

In Between DMAIC Steps: Tollgate Reviews

According to George, Rowlands and Kastle, the purpose of a tollgate review is to "Update management on the team's progress; make sure the project is still critical to the organization; adjust or re-align the project as necessary; and let management know what they can do to remove barriers for the team."[15] The institutionalization of tollgate reviews between DMAIC steps will be the backbone of your organization's continuous improvement mindset. By requiring everyone involved in the sourcing initiative to pause in between DMAIC steps, to talk to each other and to talk to company executives, the tollgate reviews ensure that services globalization is never sent to the backburner to get cold.

A continuously running DMAIC process not only allows for faithful monitoring, but also allows for changes that are made based on experience. It's true that a large number of data and facts—the foundation of Six Sigma—should be gathered prior to the launch of the global sourcing initiative. But many will come through experience. Developing a playbook—an after-the-fact set of data, facts and successful methodologies after your first initiative can be a critical step in improving the process the second time around.

---

14   George, Rowlands and Kastle, 75.
15   George, Rowlands and Kastle, 53.

Conducting the Health Check

The Six Sigma methodologies, including DMAIC, can be used to enable continuous improvement in your services globalization initiatives. One of the globalization-specific tools we've developed to specifically assess services globalization initiatives is the health check.

Just as our doctors encourage us to come in for annual exams—even if we feel perfectly healthy—so should a company regularly conduct a services globalization health check. The health check will measure output on a variety of factors and compare those measurements to established benchmarks, goals and expectations.

Conducting a health check is a way to use Six Sigma principles to measure the relative health of a globalization initiative. The health check can benefit you at a number of different points in the globalization lifecycle:

- Prior to completion of the sourcing phase of the lifecycle, you can use the health check to assess your organization's readiness for globalization and to assess proposed contracts.

- Post-transition, you can use the health check to ensure that the service management and governance arrangements are working and positioned to adapt to future changes.

- Midway through the initiative, you can use the health check to refresh your relationship with the supplier, processes, pricing and contracts.

The health check can also be useful when it comes time to renew the contract; to enable appropriate contract revisions or to terminate the agreement and set up cross- or reverse-transitioning.

A health check that is conducted objectively using rigorous Six Sigma methods can open your organization to numerous opportunities, including returns on competitiveness, human capital, delivery and technology efficiencies, and investment. Table 1 details these potential returns, and the specific activities necessary within the health check to open up the organization to these returns.

Table 6: Health Check Activities and Benefits

	Health check activity	Benefits
Return on competitiveness	▪ Conduct a portfolio assessment ▪ Evaluate delivery model choice ▪ Secure executive sponsorship ▪ Assess contract terms	▪ The alignment of globalization and business strategies ▪ The validation of the offshore strategy, or change to a more successful one ▪ Effective governance for flexibility as well as control ▪ Business model is flexible
Return on human capital	▪ Evaluate training policies and procedures ▪ Evaluate workload distribution across geographically dispersed resources ▪ Review retention strategies ▪ Conduct performance reviews ▪ Define recognition programs	▪ Match training with business needs ▪ Manage overtime ▪ Optimize resource allocation ▪ Attrition management at middle-management levels ▪ Re-confirm brand strength for recruiting ▪ Opportunity creation and internal enhancements ▪ Expansions of roles/job descriptions ▪ Individual performance management linked to corporate goals

Return on delivery efficiencies	▪ Assess transition efficiency ▪ Understand work process flow for offshore delivery ▪ Analyze trends in service levels ▪ Review quality assurance process improvements ▪ Review volume forecasting and resource allocation programs	▪ Identify weaknesses in transition model ▪ Identify areas for productivity and process improvement ▪ Recommend changes to resource utilization and work scheduling
Return on technology efficiencies	▪ Evaluate data security implementation ▪ Review data security privilege management policies ▪ Assess disaster recovery and business continuity readiness ▪ Review network and bandwidth utilization and scalability	▪ Data security methods aligned with best practices ▪ Future growth is planned ▪ Enhanced bandwidth utilization and optimization ▪ Infrastructure is flexible
Return on financial investment	▪ Evaluate savings realization ▪ Review the total cost of offshoring, including productivity and volumes	▪ Set realistic financial objectives ▪ Analyze readiness for next level of expansion ▪ Reduction and management of rework ▪ Enhanced workspace utilization ▪ Scalability enhancements and decreased time-to-market

Just as the doctor in your annual physical exam will look into your eyes, ears, nose, listen to your heart, and check your reflexes, so should you examine multiple facets of the globalization initiative. We (at Neo Advisory) have identified five areas that are important to examine during the health check: strategy, people, operations, technology, and compliance.

Strategy

The first part of the health check involves asking: Does this services globalization initiative help us meet our strategic and operational goals? Specifically, the organization should consider the following questions:

- How does the initiative support the organization's strategic goals?
- Is there a cultural fit between the organization and its suppliers?
- Do we (client and supplier) have a shared vision of the steady state?
- Have the executive sponsors remained supportive and visible?
- Has the globalization team correctly identified and prioritized our portfolio of services?

People

The second part of the health check involves asking: Are the required people and performance expectations appropriate and effective? Specifically, the organization should consider the following questions:

- Are the onsite and offsite delivery teams sufficiently staffed and skilled?
- Does the relationship between the onsite and offsite teams prevent or support what needs to be done?
- Is there an appropriate performance-based strategy?
- How does the planning for professional growth of team members compare to industry benchmarks?
- Are the required mentoring-from-a-distance processes effective for managing without local knowledge?

Operations

The third part of the health check involves asking: Is the governance structure effective and does it meet the needs of both operations? Specifically, the organization should consider the following questions:

- Is the governance structure in line with current best practices?

- Has the global delivery model been implemented across the operations?

- Are the retained organization and governance processes sufficient and effective?

- Does the globalization contract have a performance-based strategy for credits and incentives?

- Has the organization been able to move smoothly through the transition strategy? Is the strategy flexible to accommodate changes?

- Is the work process flow documented and understood across geographies?

Technology

The fourth part of the health check involves asking: Are the technology infrastructure, disaster recovery, and business continuity plans appropriate and effective? Specifically, the organization should consider the following questions:

- Do the supplier's available networking and bandwidth capabilities meet our business needs?

- How do the supplier's redundancy and latency fit with our requirements and business objectives?

- Do we have a plan for future expansion?

- Do the specified access controls (both IT and physical) meet our standards?

- Are the disaster recovery and business continuity plans in line with our requirements?

- Are we satisfied with current operational and strategic controls?

Compliance

The fifth part of the health check involves asking: Do the delivered services meet our business requirements? Are they in line with the original agreement? Specifically, the organization should consider the following questions:

- Does the current contract meet our business needs?

- Do current service levels meet our business needs?

- How does the current pricing agreement compare to current market pricing?

- Are the monitoring and governance processes complementing business needs and not hindering effective management?

- Is our data security policy being met?

- Are regulatory requirements being met?

Scoring the Health Check

When you objectively measure your performance on each of the health check areas (using the Six Sigma techniques detailed at the beginning of this chapter), you'll want to rank how well the initiative has performed in each given area.

For example, the main question to consider in the strategy part of the health check is: Does this services globalization initiative help us meet our strategic and operational goals? If an objective analysis reveals that the initiative strongly helps your strategic and operational goals, give yourself a 5; if the initiative only somewhat helps, give yourself a 3; if the initiative doesn't help at all, give yourself a 1.

Once you've objectively assessed and ranked the initiative's performance in all five of the health check categories, you'll need to assign weights to each ranking, which allow for the different relative importance of each category. Assign a 10% weight to the strategy and technology categories; assign a 20% weight to the operations category; and assign 30% weights to the people and compliance categories. Using those weighted rankings you can determine an overall ranking of your globalization initiative's health.

Case Example: Ongoing Success from Successful Globalization

A Fortune 500 computer, networking and communications products manufacturer is an example of a company that has found ongoing success in services globalization. The technology company was one of the first to seriously consider sourcing to global locations. It realized that with India's low-cost base and large availability of skilled talent, sourcing support work to India could generate significant cost savings for the company. So the company set up a captive center in India.

After successfully sourcing support work to its captive center in India, the technology company began to think about other processes it could source globally. Could it go beyond the traditionally offshored support processes to globally source higher value-added processes as well? The company's experience with highly qualified resources in India suggested that it could, indeed, benefit from sourcing higher valued-added processes.

So that's what the company did: it began globally sourcing processes such as testing, and even research and development. Now, captive centers in India and other countries play a key role in the development of the company's core technology products.

But it was only by way of its continuous improvement mindset that the company asked itself: could we be doing even better? The company continues to look for new ways that it can leverage services globalization to improve business efficiency. Currently, the company conducts almost a quarter of its research and development outside the U.S., in countries such as India, Russia, Malaysia, and China.

The Ends Over Means

One of the most common mistakes that client organizations make is seeing services globalization as an end rather than a means. Applying the principles of Six Sigma to services globalization reminds us that global sourcing is actually the means to an end—an end that is, ultimately, serving our customers needs well.

The purpose of embracing a continuous improvement mindset in services globalization is to allow for continuous gains. If you follow the processes outlined in the other chapters of this book, you'd probably have a successful initiative, even without adopting a continuous improvement mindset. But your gains would be one-time.

To realize continuous gains, adopt a continuous improvement mindset: never stop learning, use the define-measure-analyze-improve-control model, conduct regular health checks, and always keep a lookout for new opportunities to do better.

And remember, in Six Sigma founder Dr. Deming's words, "If you can't describe what you are doing as a process, you don't know what you're doing."

Secret #7: Embrace a Continuous Improvement Mindset: Key Points

- Embracing a continuous improvement mindset throughout the lifecycle of the global initiative will allow the organization to understand how well the initiative is working.

- Successful globalizers leverage their global initiatives for business transformation (including process improvement) but understand that if processes are flawed because of the institutionalized way of doing things within the organization; simply shipping a few back-office processes overseas will not solve the problem.

- Six Sigma teaches that to improve their businesses, organizations must look at the causes of their problems—and fix those causes in order to remedy the problems.

- The health check is a globalization-specific way to use Six Sigma principles to measure the relative health of a globalization initiative. The health check can benefit the organization at a number of different points in the globalization lifecycle, including:

  - Prior to completion of the sourcing phase of the lifecycle, the organization can use the health check to assess its readiness for globalization and to assess proposed contracts.

  - Post-transition, organizations can use the health check to ensure that the service management and governance arrangements are working and positioned to adapt to future changes.

  - Midway through the initiative, the health check can be used to refresh the organization's relationships with the suppler, processes, pricing, and contracts.

  - When it comes time to renew the contract; to enable appropriate contract revisions or to terminate the agreement and set up cross- or reverse-transitioning.

- A health check that is conducted objectively using rigorous Six Sigma methods can open the organization to numerous opportunities, including returns on competitiveness, human capital, delivery and technology efficiencies, and investment.

Beyond Successful Globalizing: The Futurized Corporation

It's been over a decade since corporations started leveraging outsourcing to better manage capacity, costs, quality, risk and speed to market. From offshoring to managed services, there has been a dramatic evolution in corporations' thinking about outsourcing. Corporations are challenging existing business models as they seek ways to speed innovation, focus on their core competencies, and scale to capitalize on opportunities and outpace competitors. Today, many corporations are looking beyond back-office, labor-intensive tasks to outsource more complex business processes – from investment and pricing analytics to inventory management to aircraft engine maintenance forecasting. It is no longer a debate as to whether to outsource but rather what functions can be outsourced. As a business consultant, I hear often about companies' abilities to achieve cost and/or capacity advantages, and yet, many are still not satisfied. For some, it has not given them much advantage from a competitive standpoint and for others it is just moving the "cost" around. I hear often from businesses, when will I see significant value?

It is not hard to understand why the question of value is still raised when you consider that today's outsourcing models have some inherent limitations that reduce the overall gains companies can achieve: low worker retention, lack of control and visibility for clients, and long, inflexible agreements to cover execution and investment risks for both parties. These issues are more pronounced due to recent trends in internet and social networking capabilities that have us rethinking outsourcing from a geography game (i.e. "cheap labor force") to a game of skill and expertise (i.e. recruiting a team of all-star experts). Few business "futurist" or industry pundits would argue that the popularity of social networking, collaboration tools and the pervasiveness of Web-based applications from email to CRM have given corporations greater visibility, control, and speed than ever before. We have become accustomed to "always on" services and give little thought to the backend processes that deliver those applications to our laptop – it just happens. It is what many people today refer to as "cloud computing." I believe there is a lot of value in an outsourcing model that borrows a page from cloud computing - on-demand, pay-as-you-go, unbound by geographic constraints, and where tasks are assigned to a team of distributed workers. Seriously, what's not to like? I call this next phase in outsourcing, "cloudsourcing."

Cloudsourcing combines on-demand business process outsourcing (BPO) with crowdsourcing technologies to enable companies to purchase quality BPO services on-demand through a pay-per-use model. Cloudsourcing allows corporations to launch new business process work types, scale and innovate in Internet time and maintain real-time visibility and control to minimize risk. Further, it enables corporations to have immediate access to the right worker, with the right skill, at the appropriate price point, regardless of location.

For those in the consulting world, there is no doubt that the world is truly flat as Thomas Friedman presented so vividly in his book. With cloudsourcing, "The Flat World" becomes more visible and the creation of on-demand workforce can be realized. Imagine being able to hire what skills you want, when you want and for how long you want! This not only converts your fixed costs to a variable structure but also enables you to launch new programs in internet speed -- broadband, of course! Cloudsourcing also enables BPOs and individuals who have particular skills or expertise new avenues to offer their services on-demand.

So when will cloudsourcing be a reality? Interestingly, there are examples of work being deployed in this model today. Take for instance, LiveOps, a Silicon Valley technology company run by Maynard Webb, the former Chief Operating Officer of eBay. It has been cloudsourcing through a virtual workforce of more than 20,000 independent contractors, and recently launched a new work marketplace, LiveWork, as a platform for on-demand business process outsourcing. While the company provides on-demand contact center services to a wide range of businesses, the impact of cloudsourcing is best illustrated with the services they provide with natural disaster emergency relief efforts where fast response to the "unpredictable" is the norm:

> When Hurricane Katrina hit the Gulf Coast of the U.S. in 2005, a toll-free communications center was urgently needed to put victims in touch with their families. Every other outsourcer that was approached to provide communications services declined to take on the project, because they couldn't mobilize agents fast enough. Within three hours, LiveOps launched a call center with over 300 independent, home-based agents ready to help reunite victims of Hurricane Katrina with their family members. The virtual call center, with no fixed investment in buildings or technology infrastructure, was established with skilled workers in hours and then subsequently wound down when work was done.

Consider what all of this may mean for your business or industry - a retailer during its high season being able to scale to meet call volumes, a technology company needing to rapidly staff up its email customer support team in response to a new product release, , or a gaming company needing an on-demand workforce to augment their existing team to help moderate their online chatrooms. I believe the possibilities are huge and will lead to more work types being outsourced.

In the summer of 2007, I wrote an article titled "Futurized Corporation," describing a company that shines in its ability to seamlessly stitch together component-based, composable services from different providers and its own operations to re-create self-standing business functions – i.e. a virtualized services supply chain. This vision is cloudsourcing at its best. I believe with this new trend, companies now may be able to achieve significant gains by taking advantage of the on-demand BPO model that increases velocity and agility and thus creates sustainable competitive advantage.

The successful globalizers and leaders I've outlined in this book are already looking beyond their successes in sourcing globally. They're looking for the next advantage, the next competitive edge. That edge, I believe, will be the ability to seamlessly stitch together component-based services from different providers and in-house operations to recreate self-standing business functions; a virtualized supply chain.

This is the Futurized Corporation.

Clearly, there has already been a dramatic evolution in corporations' thinking about outsourcing. But as far as services globalization has evolved, the question for today's corporation nevertheless remains: "Which functions should be outsourced?"

The Futurized Corporation, in contrast, asks: "How can I better serve my stakeholders? Can I leverage services globalization to make it happen?" Instead of considering certain processes that can be chosen to be sourced, the Futurized Corporation focuses on the stakeholders and leverages services globalization to achieve goals. It also focuses on what its core competency is and what it leverages others to complete its quilt.

Broadly, the Futurized Corporation will keep three pieces in-house: its vision, strategic execution and core competencies. These three building blocks will be the sources of competitive advantage for the Futurized Corporation—beyond them, all functions in the value chain can be outsourced and done better by others.

The Futurized Corporation's vision is a plan for what the business will look like in 5, 20—even 100—years. The organization knows the kind of business it wants to be, the partners it wants to engage and the customers it wants to serve.

A key part of becoming a futurized corporation is flexibility. The concept of the futurized corporation is about being ready for any change that could happen in the market—it's the ultimate in flexibility.

That's a sentiment echoed by Ron Kifer, Group VP and CIO at Applied Materials. "Organizations need a business platform that is agile and can accommodate changes in the competitive landscape. No matter how successful you are today—with your strategy, with your product, with your customers, what you can expect is that things will change very dramatically tomorrow. You need to be flexible in where you do business and with whom you do business—with your strategic relationships."

So strategic execution includes the corporation's ability to engage and disengage sourced services quickly and effectively and its ability to seamlessly integrate services from different providers to re-create self-standing business functions (the virtual supply chain). These abilities will be key to the Futurized Corporation's success after it has completely shed all but its most core competitive advantage functions.

The Futurized Corporation's core includes those competencies or assets that cannot be separated from the corporation without fundamentally changing it, including, perhaps, entrepreneurial capabilities, intellectual property, goodwill, relationships, values, principles, reputation and brand.

Not only will the Futurized Corporation outsource what corporations today consider core, but it will actually redefine what is core. Some corporations are already headed on that path. EA (Electronic Arts), for example, outsources art asset development—a critical component of the creative development process (which intuitively would appear a core function for a game developer). And Nike, too, outsources a large percentage of its non-core functions, retaining primarily brand ownership and design—the one function that Nike truly considers core.

It may seem counterintuitive that companies like Nike and EA would outsource seemingly core activities like product design or creative development. But they're good examples of how the companies that will become futurized corporations see core competencies in a different way—they are at the forefront of the paradigm shift in how companies think about what is core.

By virtualizing its services supply chain—engaging and disengaging service providers quickly and effectively to seamlessly stitch together services—the Futurized Corporation is able to offer its customers more of what they demand, including customer-centric and customized products and services.

Dell, for example, allows its customers to build their own computer on its website, which allows the company to create a unique product for each individual customer—and Dell's virtualized supply chain makes the whole process cost-effective (the company leverages economies of sourcing). In that way, Dell is able to maintain direct touch with its customers, effectively owning the customer experience.

Driving Futurization: The Service-Oriented Business Architecture Concept

The driver that will allow the evolution toward the Futurized Corporation is the emergence of service providers within a service-oriented business architecture. The concept of service oriented business architecture (SOBA) is borrowed from service-oriented architecture (SOA), which encompasses technology-based services such as e-commerce. The principle behind SOA and SOBA is that a company uses what exists, integrating its own resources with purchased, pre-packaged resources from others.

One SOA technology, for example, is the payment gateway—the Web equivalent of credit-card process machines at retail stores. Payment gateways are built by banks that then share the technology with online merchants. By stitching together banks' payment gateways with its own website—whether it's a site that sells items or one that accepts online bill payments—a merchant is able to offer its customers a service they demand—online payment—without having to invent and build that payment system itself.

But a service-oriented business architecture by itself is not sufficient to allow the development of the Futurized Corporation; there needs to be service providers available to offer the kinds of services that the Futurized Corporation needs to be able to create a virtual value chain.

Already, the trend is toward a world in which there are plenty of competent external suppliers at every level of the value chain. A greater number of providers in increasingly larger parts of the world are offering a broader range of more complex services today than five or ten years ago—eight years from now, there should be ample supply of service providers competent at all levels of the supply chain.

Those service providers will be diversified in what they do and where they operate from, but they will all have certain characteristics in common:

- Each service provider will offer a particular service that matches the Futurized Corporation's compartmentalized service needs (for example, the payroll processing component of a company's HR function).

- Service providers will be highly focused. Just as the Futurized Corporation retains only its vision, core, and strategic execution, so will the service providers focus on their own way of serving their customers and outsource all non-core functions.

- They will work under standard interface definitions so that the Futurized Corporation can seamlessly stitch together services from multiple providers.

- Their operations will be encapsulated, or "black-boxed"—they will be outside of the Futurized Corporation's view except during due diligence prior to contract signing and during periodic audits. (For this reason, service agreements and contracts will be crucial to successful interactions in a SOBA-based future.)

Snapshot: Virtualized Services Supply Chains

To truly understand the evolution of a corporation from its present to its futurized state, it's helpful to take a look at how each business function may be done globally in the Futurized Corporation—and how those futurized business functions look different from today's or yesterday's. Imagine all of an organization's business functions and ask, "How will services globalization and the virtualization of the supply chain change these business functions?"

Customer Service for a Bank

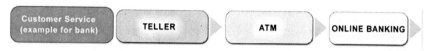

Banks have been able to offer more customized customer service by evolving from teller-based customer service to an online banking self-service model. While mass customized in the true sense, a bank's website allows customers to tailor their experiences to their own needs and preferences. And unlike teller- and ATM-based customer service, with online banking, the customer's fulfillment process isn't pre-structured by the bank; the customer drives his own need-fulfillment process, navigating the website based on what he wants and needs.

IT for a Consumer Goods Company

Ten years ago, companies began to replace legacy applications with packaged software solutions and hired service providers to implement, maintain and support those packages. In the future, that Application Service Provider (ASP) model will evolve to a software-as-service model as service providers offer software on their servers for rent to corporations. Where the corporation of the past made its own software solutions, the corporation of the present buys them, and the Futurized Corporation will pay for them on a per-use basis.

At the same time as the software procurement has evolved, so have the types of IT functions that companies outsource. As IT has evolved within the corporation, service providers have moved up the value chain; now they are able to provide more than skills, including the ability to take on and manage application maintenance, development and support projects.

Human Resources for a Telecommunications Company

Services globalization allows organizations to customize their product/service offerings. In HR, for example, the present corporation already shows the beginnings of the customization trend, with self-service employee portals. Self-service is a key characteristic that we'll continue to see more of in HR as corporations futurize.

And while the corporation of the present shows the beginnings of HR virtualization, it is in the evolution to the Futurized Corporation that the HR supply chain becomes completely virtualized. In the Futurized Corporation, the HR function will have only one employee: the HR outsourcing manager who works with service providers to cover the outsourced value chain, ensuring that each process is seamlessly stitched together.

Game Development for a Gaming Company

The game development company of the past did all of its development in-house. Modern game development companies began outsourcing with simple game testing, then outsourced minor game modifications, then simple art assets (objects such as tables, chairs, etc.), and then more complex art assets (including texturing, modeling and animation). Today's game development company outsources those processes as well as character development.

But the futurized game development company will outsource the entire game development function (including logic). That will bring the company to its core, with conceptualization and design alone being done in-house.

Investment Analytics for an Investment Bank

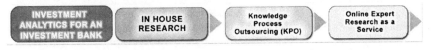

The investment bank of the past performed all of its investment analytics internally. Today, many investment banks outsource the knowledge-gathering process, but the futurized investment bank will seek out online expertise sold by research vendors—the bank can either buy the vendor's pre-packaged research or commission-customized research from the vendor. But the research itself will no longer be a key differentiator for investment banks—what they do with the research, what they take from it, will be the new competitive advantage.

Getting from Here to There: Creating a Futurization Road Map

In order to evolve from the present corporation toward the futurized corporation, organizations must develop a clear roadmap for aligning themselves toward the future. That roadmap has five steps.

Step 1: Assess SOBA Readiness

The first step that an organization must take on the path to becoming a Futurized Corporation is to assess its readiness to deal with the business world in the future. The organization must ask, "Are we ready to take advantage of the opportunities provided by the evolving global economy?" Most importantly, corporations will have to learn how to leverage SOBA.

Step 2: Develop a Services Globalization Competency

As the Futurized Corporation sheds all of its non-core business functions, retaining only its vision, core and strategic leadership, it will have to hone its ability to successfully source around the virtualized services supply chain. To do that, the Futurized Corporation must develop competencies in sourcing, governing and managing strategic alliances with its service providers; the old model of deriving competitive advantage from business functions like research and development or sales and marketing will no longer apply in the future.

Step 3: Restructure as a Utility Operational Model

To accomplish the goal of compartmentalization and unit-level economic feasibility, the corporation must organize its business around the utility services concept— sharing a common infrastructure on commodity processes, sometimes even with competitors. Then, not only must each business function be economically feasible, but it must also contribute to the organization's greater vision for the future; if it can't, the organization should take that individual function out of the value chain and outsource it to a provider that can provide the service more efficiently.

Step 4: Virtualize the Services Supply Chain

If an organization's business functions will all be virtualized—outsourced individually to different service providers—then an organization must become prepared to source its processes that way by compartmentalizing internally first. To become ready for the future, organizations must break every function up as a profit and loss account—every department and every function will be accountable for its economic feasibility.

Step 5: Leverage the Economic Value of the Service Network

Where internal providers do provide services for the Futurized Corporation, they will have to behave like external providers, offering clearly defined service agreements and maintaining cost competitiveness. They'll have to "share the pain and share the gain." They will be "paid" with credits against their profit and loss accounts. And they will have to compete with external service providers for the job—they must be able to offer the Futurized Corporation a value that the external providers can't in order to remain in-house (and the onus is on the internal providers to periodically prove that value).

Case Study: Virgin Mobile USA

Virgin Mobile USA is a good example of a company on its way to becoming a futurized corporation. Virgin Mobile USA understands its strengths, makes those strengths its core functions, focuses on those core functions, and outsources the rest. The company, launched in 2002, is a joint venture between Virgin Group and Sprint Nextel; it is the first Mobile Virtual Network Operator (MVNO) in the U.S. and the first mobile telecommunications company in the U.S. to focus exclusively on the youth market.

As an MVNO, Virgin Mobile USA does not own its network structure; instead, it purchases minutes from Sprint's network to resell under the Virgin brand. In a May 2002 article in *Telecommunications International*, Tom Alexander, then CEO and managing director of Virgin Mobile, said, "The brand is our biggest asset because it symbolizes the great customer experience that Virgin stands for." Instead of trying to be good at operating a network infrastructure *and* maintaining its brand, Virgin Mobile opted to stick to what it's good at—maintaining its brand—and develop a relationship with another company that could offer the other piece.

But its MVNO structure is not the only way that Virgin Mobile USA embodies many of the characteristics of a futurized corporation. It also outsources processes and functions that aren't truly core (its brand is a large part of Virgin Mobile USA's core). The company enlisted the help of third-party providers to design, implement and manage new interactive voice response (IVR) systems, including a Spanish IVR to help the company increase its market share among Spanish-speaking consumers.

Virgin Mobile USA also chose to purchase a service oriented architecture (SOA) system to integrate and manage its operations—including point-of-sale order processing, product fulfillment, service provisioning and connectivity with the Sprint network. That SOA system allowed Virgin Mobile USA to launch operations only seven months after the company was created and allows the company to continue to roll out new features about every four weeks.

Transforming Today's Corporations into Tomorrow's Futurizers

In order to work toward becoming a futurized corporation—one that quickly and effectively engages and disengages service components to seamlessly stitch together services and create a virtualized supply chain—today's corporation must ask:

- Do we have a clear vision of the future? What would our business world will be like?

- How will we fit in that world?

- Do we recognize what it takes to get to that vision?

- What role does services globalization play in this?

- Have we started working towards it?

The process of becoming a futurized corporation is a journey rather than a destination. But it's a journey that will allow the organization to grow by focusing on what's truly core.

Happy Journey!

ABOUT THE AUTHOR

Atul Vashistha is a leading proponent and practitioner of globalization and futurizing enterprises. He has two decades of global business expertise and founded Neo Advisory (Formerly neoIT) in 1999 with the mission of helping enterprises grow their business and improve operations by capitalizing on services globalization. This passion for globalization of services and a unique business model has helped neoIT establish itself as the leader in the services globalization advisory and management arena. This has also led to Atul being recognized globally for his thought leadership and experience is the global services economy. In 2007, Atul founded NEOGROUP to help companies optimize major programs and governance. NEOGROUP provides best practices and resources to monitor, report and optimize major programs and governance. In 2009, Atul founded Best Outsourcing Jobs and Global Ability to further fuel the global services economy and develop a stronger global services supply chain. All these firms operate under his Globalization Wisdom Group.

Atul's opinions are valued by media and wall street analysts such as CNN, ABCNews, CNBC, ITAA, SIG, Outsourcing World Summit, HRO World, Merrill Lynch, Goldman Sachs, Fortune, Forbes, Business Week, Wall Street Journal, Investors Business Daily, Economist, CIO and other global organizations. Atul continues to be a vocal proponent of globalization and has taken on the critics, such as Lou Dobbs and his "Exporting America" segment on CNN. He has co-authored a book published by McGraw Hill in January 2006 on services globalization titled, "The Offshore Nation" which focuses on the services globalization mega-trend and its economic and human impact on nations and firms. His next book, The 7 Secrets of Great Globalizers is likely to be published by Spring 2010. Atul also writes an ongoing column for HRO Today, FAO Today and Outsourcing Malaysia. He is also a frequent contributor to other magazines such as CIO, Global Services and Business Finance.

Consulting Magazine named Atul as one of the "Top 25 Most Influential Consultants" in 2006 and "Top 6 IT Powerbrokers" in 2004. HRO Today named Atul as a HR Outsourcing Superstar five years in a row from 2004 through 2009. FAO Today named him a Superstar in 2007 and 2008. Arizona State University honored him as a "Distinguished Alumni".

He serves on the Boards of IDEA, Center for Services Leadership at Arizona State University, IAOP, Defense Business Board and Neo Group. He is also active with the global non-profit network of entrepreneurs, TiE, Silicon Valley where he is a Charter Member and Chair of the "Cross Border Services CxO Forum". Atul is also a member and board member of the Northern California chapter of YPO and a mentor to the Stanford University's Reuters Digital Vision Fellow Program.

Prior to neoIT, Atul was at Cardinal Health (NYSE: CAH) as Senior Vice President of International, he led the international operations of the Fortune 25 Company. Atul and his seasoned team at Cardinal expanded profitable operations to Australia, New Zealand, Spain, UK, Singapore, Brazil, Mexico, Japan and other global locations. More importantly, his in-depth international experience earned him the admiration and respect of global CEOs, business leaders and government officials.

Atul and his firms are redefining how nations create competitive advantage in global services and how firms and individuals can leverage this mega-trend to build better futures for all. Further details can be found at www.google.com (search for Atul Vashistha). He can also be reached at atul@globalizationwisdom.com.

LaVergne, TN USA
11 May 2010
182393LV00001B/8/P